WA.
Uni
ma
His
wit
On
yea
Cer

of t
Th
Pat
De
fou
plu
Wo

at t

ourgh
subtle
nomic
rades
ding.
or 20
tudies

rman
le for
ys on
f Red
s the
ooks,
to the

arwin

As the younger Old Red Sandstone lies on top of the older Silurian rocks at Siccar Point, so does the title page of *Origin of Species* (3rd edition, 1844) overlie the title page of *Vestiges of Creation* (1st edition, 1844)

ON

THE ORIGIN OF SPECIES

BY MEANS OF NATURAL SELECTION,

OR THE

PRESERVATION OF FAVOURED RACES IN THE STRUGGLE
FOR LIFE.

By CHARLES DARWIN, M.A.,

FELLOW OF THE ROYAL, GEOLOGICAL, LINNEAN, ETC., SOCIETIES;
AUTHOR OF 'JOURNAL OF RESEARCHES DURING H. M. S. BEAGLE'S VOYAGE ROUND THE WORLD.'

THIRD EDITION, WITH ADDITIONS AND CORRECTIONS.

(*SEVENTH THOUSAND.*)

LONDON:
JOHN MURRAY, ALBEMARLE STREET.
1861.

The right of Translation is reserved.

VESTIGES

OF

THE NATURAL HISTORY

OF

CREATION.

LONDON:
JOHN CHURCHILL, PRINCES STREET, SOHO.
MDCCCXLIV.

Contrast the light and sparse nature of *Vestiges* – with no indication of authorship – with the weighty and tendentious title of *Origin* and the establishment of its author's authority.

The Evolution of Evolution

Darwin, Enlightenment and Scotland

WALTER STEPHEN

Luath Press Limited

EDINBURGH

www.luath.co.uk

First published 2009

ISBN: 978-1-906817-23-7

The paper used in this book is recyclable. It is made from low
chlorine pulps produced in a low energy, low emission manner from
renewable forests.

The publishers acknowledge the support of

Scottish
Arts Council

towards the publication of this volume.

Printed and bound by
Bell & Bain Ltd., Glasgow

Typeset in 11 point Sabon by
3btype.com

Contents

Illustrations – Figures

Acknowledgements

THE AUTHOR IS INDEBTED to Professor Aubrey Manning, Emeritus Professor of Natural History, University of Edinburgh, for suggesting him for a project which made for an enjoyable winter, and to Professor Susan Manning of the Institute for Advanced Studies in the Humanities, University of Edinburgh for encouragement to proceed. So much is known and so much has been written about Darwin – for example, Marc Giraud's bibliography cites over a hundred books in French – that one has to poke around in obscure corners to come up with anything new that is worth sharing.

Staff in the great national institutions have been supportive beyond the call of duty. Rhoda Fothergill, doyenne of the Perthshire Society for Natural Science, has helped to illuminate a Darwin core-periphery relationship. Bob Mitchell, leader of botanical explorations, opened my eyes in Chile. Philip Stone, of the Edinburgh Geological Society, ironed out a few prejudices, while Mrs Lloyd helped to locate Darwin's much-decayed Malvern bolt-hole. Anne-Michelle Slater, of the University of Aberdeen, created opportunities for sharpening up inchoate thoughts.

The cover of *A Most Unsettling Person: An Introduction to the Ideas and Life of Patrick Geddes,* by Paddy Kitchen, is reproduced as Fig 18 by kind permission of the publisher, Victor Gollancz, an imprint of the Orion Publishing Group. The map extract of part of Glen Roy (Fig 12) and the sketch of Glen Roy from Chambers, *Ancient Sea Margins* (Fig 15) are reproduced by kind permission of the National Library of Scotland. The Frontispiece reproduces the title pages of *Vestiges of Creation* and *Origin of Species*, again by kind permission of the National Library of Scotland. 'Terror' (Fig 16) is reproduced by kind permission of The Folio Society. The Appendix from *Who's Who 1930* is reproduced by kind permission of A&C Black Publishers Ltd.

The clear diagrams and map (Figs 3–6 and Fig 14) are by Olrig Stephen.

CHAPTER ONE

Darwin and his Mentors

THE CELEBRATION OF anniversaries has become big business and, at its mid-point, 2009 promises to be another good year for the anniversary business. It is a special anniversary year for many interesting and important people, such as Burns, Haydn and Mendelssohn. Burns wrote of his own birthday (25 January 1759) when the gable end of his parents' house collapsed in a gale:

> Our monarch's hinmost year but ane
> 　　Was five-and-twenty days begun,
> 'Twas then a blast o' Janwar' Win'
> 　　Blew hansel in on Robin.

In November 1785, on turning up a mouse's nest with the plough, he opened up the whole question of Man's relationship with his fellow-creatures:

> I'm truly sorry Man's dominion
> Has broken Nature's social union.

In his sentimental poet's way he might even seem to be apologising for the Book of Genesis in which Man was created separately from and superior to the remainder of Creation.

Haydn's death in 1809 brought to an end a great stream of tuneful and apparently straightforward music. Modern programme-makers love him because he wrote 104 symphonies and there are 52 weeks in the year.

One of Haydn's sidelines was to write arrangements of Scots songs for George Thomson, an Edinburgh publisher, among them some of the songs we now think of as by Burns. These are by no means Haydn's best work and must be thought of as potboilers. But *The Creation* is a great work of faith and optimism. According to *The Oxford Companion to Music*, 'It is naïve but charming, and admirably reflects the simple devotion of its author' who said he 'knelt down daily and prayed God to strengthen me for it.' Haydn's *Creation* is straight out of Genesis but much of it sounds like a musical foretaste of the much-quoted passage from Darwin's *Envoy:*

> There is a grandeur in this view of life, with its several powers, having been originally breathed by the Creator into a few forms, or into one; and that... from so simple a beginning endless forms most beautiful and most wonderful have been, and are being, evolved.

Mendelssohn was a 20-year-old celebrity when he visited Scotland in 1829. *Fingal's Cave* or the *Hebrides Overture* is much more than a simple souvenir of a happy holiday; more, even, than a simple sound picture of the waves rolling up the beach. Mendelssohn was probably the first to convey effectively through music the grandeur of natural forces and the puniness of Man when set beside them. Again, we can see in some of his work the kind of emotion experienced by Darwin in La Campana, Chile.

In the middle of the year and turning to Charles Darwin, 2009 has a double significance. It is the 200th anniversary of his birth, on 12 February 1809 and on 24 November 1859 was published one of the most influential and disturbing books of all time. The title page called it: *On the Origin of Species by Means of Natural Selection, or the Preservation of Favoured Races in the Struggle for Life*. The first five words are bland enough, but the next phrase is controversial and the latter half of the title is downright provocative. It could be that more people have learnt about their selves and their relationship with the natural world through *The Origin of Species* than via the combined efforts of the other great men we celebrate in 2009.

One recalls 1970, the year in which the Council of Europe decided that the 200th anniversary of the birth of Beethoven be celebrated through-out Western Europe. At the time I thought this quite unnecessary, after all, Beethoven's music was everywhere and did not need any artificial atten-tion. But I was wrong, the celebration meant that not only did we hear a lot of Beethoven, but all kinds of new relationships and forgotten works were brought into the open, for our greater enjoyment and understanding.

Do the Darwin anniversaries matter? Especially in this year? Steve Jones, Professor of Genetics, University College, London would say 'No!' His hope for Darwin Year was that:

...by its end, its subject's beard, his gastric troubles and even his voyage on HMS *Beagle* will have faded from public consciousness. I would be even happier if the squabbles about the social, moral, legal, political, historical, ethical and theological implications of his work were to find, at last, their long-delayed demise. In 2009 we should celebrate the science rather than the man – the fact rather than the anecdote.

One sees his point – Archimedes is more than a man running down the street crying 'Eureka!' and Newton did more than doze under a tree in an orchard – but there is surely a middle position.

Despite Steve Jones, there is a case for celebrating the man as well as the science, so long as celebrating the man contributes to our understanding of how he learned and thought, of the evolution of evolution and does not descend to antiquarianism and pawky anecdote. The big beard features in the work that follows, but only as an element in a scene explaining Darwin and his charisma. Gastric troubles do not rate a mention, but again and again we come up against the ambiguities and uncertainties of Darwin's relationships and can work out for ourselves what the consequences were likely to be. The *Beagle* voyage is here, but not as a travelogue. Instead, it was the setting for a basic change in attitude which was eventually to answer our biggest questions: Where do we come from? And where are we going?

An event of this kind deserves great celebration and 2009 is being marked by special programmes in the media and a rush of new books. In every university and natural history society there are lectures, seminars and audio-visual presentations. Perhaps inevitably, this coverage tends to be metropolitan and looks at Darwin at Cambridge, or in relation to the London-based scientific societies and the great London museums. Much of his working life was spent at his one-man laboratory, database and research centre 13 miles from Marble Arch at (as it says on his notepaper): 'Down[1], Beckenham, Kent. Railway Station, Orpington, South Eastern Railway.' As Desmond and Moore, Darwin's meticulous biographers, have said:

> There was no place for natural history like London, even if there was no nature in the 'odious dirty smoky' capital. London was the imperium of science.

This statement bears closer examination. Clearly we know what the authors mean. London – 'the Great Wen' – is and was the magnet for everything worthwhile and everything undesirable in the country. Until London acquired its university in 1836, there were two universities in England, both of them easily accessible from the city and each more accessible from London than from the other.

But there are at least two tendentious phrases in this rather facile quotation. As I sit, I look across at a bookshelf on which stands *London's Natural History*, by R. S. R. Fitter, 282 pages, 40 colour plates, 32 plates in black and white and 11 diagrams and maps, published in 1945. The message is clear. Nature is everywhere, from the deepest oceans almost to the tops of the highest mountains. When it is destroyed by volcanic eruption or human chemical intervention it immediately begins to recolonise the lost ground. Nowhere on Earth has 'no nature' for very long.

Later we shall see how three men made a boat journey to a lonely shore in Berwickshire in order to revolutionise how we think about the Earth and its age. That experience could be replicated in thousands of locations all over the world – given that the viewers are able to see and think clearly. London is, and was, the meeting place of scientists, where their work is published, and is the home of great research institutions – but a great deal of science is still done in the field or in certain favoured locations. In Darwin's time, if London was the imperium of science, there was at least a principality four hundred miles to the north, where Edinburgh was one of the four (five until Marischal College and King's College amalgamated in 1860) Scottish universities.

The young Darwin did not burst, perfectly formed, from the brow of some Greek goddess. His *Autobiography* tells us that he spent two unsatisfactory years at Edinburgh University and left without graduating.

At Cambridge he followed a gentleman's course which would have led to a place in the Church of England. The connections he made there led him to the voyage on the *Beagle*, the outcome of which was a career as a naturalist – a choice greatly eased with his inheritance on the death of his father. Along the way he met a series of mentors and it is with these and their relationship to Darwin that this book is concerned.

Some threads run right through the book. Today we would equate Natural History with Biology – Botany and Zoology. In Darwin's time Geology was also a part of Natural History, often the most important part.

Darwin considered himself a geologist first for quite some time after the *Beagle* cruise. Science was still in the discovery phase during Darwin's lifetime – new species of plants and animals seemed to be being found every day. These had to be identified, named and their relationships with others established. Fossils might provide evidence of change (or not). The rocks in which fossils were found had to be ordered and dated.

The turning point of the *Beagle* voyage is generally considered to be the Galapagos Islands, where Darwin observed the differences between the fauna from the different islands, to deduce that these differing populations had evolved from a common ancestor over time. Yet recording and explaining were quite separate processes, it was only after several years in England that Darwin made the necessary deductions.

Earlier, in the Chilean Andes, Darwin had stood, observed, measured and realised that the making of the mountains had taken an extremely long time. This meant that, when he came to consider the evolution of the Galapagos finches, he was able to see that process as being a long series of minute changes from generation to generation – but that there was ample time for these changes to take place. 'Deep time' was the engine for evolutionary change.

'Deep time' could get people into trouble with the authorities. The ancient universities were theocracies (London – 'The Godless Institution of Gower Street' – was not), staffed by clergy of the Church of England and open only to students subscribing to the Church of England. The Earth had been created in six days, then God rested. Man was a special creation, in that he was created in the image of God, and was made master of the rest of creation. Noah's Ark was a problem. Its dimensions were known and its capacity calculated. All other species had been eliminated in the Great Flood (these were the fossils – 'vestiges of creation') yet new species were being discovered all the time which could not possibly have been accommodated in the Ark.

To enter the church, Darwin would have had formally and publicly to subscribe to these beliefs. At Cambridge and subsequently, his mentors were the Cambridge divines, Buckland, Sedgwick and Henslow. All were senior in the Church and in the University; all were 'men of science' of some distinction and influential in the scientific community. Darwin could not afford to estrange men with such power. What was he to do?

James Joyce defined the situation of the creative artist in Ireland in the early 20th century as 'silence, cunning or exile.' Joyce chose cunning and exile. Under similar repressive pressures, Darwin chose – consciously or unconsciously – silence and a degree of cunning. Darwin was an avid networker. He wrote thousands of letters and a shelf full of solid, informative books, but he was very circumspect about his views, to the point of being secretive or deceptive. Like one of today's blogging travellers, he kept in touch with Henslow from South America, carefully easing out gradually his 'conversion' to deep time in the knowledge that Henslow would read out his letters in public and publish them.

Darwin kept journals and notes all his life: surely they must provide unambiguous evidence of his thoughts at critical points? Perhaps, but most of what appeared in the public domain was much less spontaneous than it seems. For example, Darwin kept a detailed diary during the *Beagle* voyage but it was seven months after his return to England before it was published. *Voyage of the* Beagle appeared in 1839, three years after her return. There was clearly ample opportunity for massaging the text to fit the conclusions.

Darwin did not wish to antagonise, nor did he wish to offend. His wife, Emma, was comfortably domestic and of simple faith. We are told that Darwin would do nothing that would distress her. Secrecy and ambiguity became a way of life and must, I believe, have been responsible for his ill-health, the cause of which is still an unresolved issue among the medical profession.

In episodes from the life of Darwin, I am now about to describe and analyse the contribution made to Darwin's development by a series of mentors, starting with the rigorous basic training which qualified him for independent research work and provided the building blocks for his work on evolution and natural selection. Light is also thrown on some vexing questions. Why did Darwin denigrate his Edinburgh experiences? Why did he seem to be unaware of the concept of 'deep time'? Why did he seem to undervalue mentors who did so much for him?

For evolution to work and for natural selection to operate an enormously long time-scale was necessary – a recent broadcast I half overheard suggested that a mere 100,000 generations would have been enough for the simplest fossil eye to move its position and to evolve into something like our own fairly sophisticated eye! To a historian 100,000 generations seems an inordinately long time but 100,000 human generations is only two million years. The Old Red Sandstone at Siccar Point was laid down about 400 million years ago, allowing abundant opportunity for what was called in Darwin's day 'transmutation'.

In 1788 Dr James Hutton of Edinburgh, at Siccar Point, gave a field demonstration of the immensity of time. He said: 'We find no vestige of a beginning, no prospect of an end.' Yet Stephen Baxter, in *Revolutions in the Earth* (2003), can say:

> In the 19th century even Charles Darwin would graduate from Cambridge University believing that the world was six thousand years old, give or take.

Matthew Bramble, in Smollett's *Humphry Clinker* of 1771, described the Edinburgh of his time as 'a hotbed of genius'. How did Darwin, in two years in an Edinburgh still shaped by the Enlightenment, manage to avoid the concept of 'deep time' and its consequences? And why, when the concept was eventually absorbed by him, had it come the long way round?

Charles Lyell (1797–1875) was a keen young geologist in 1824, and was taken to Hutton's Unconformity at Siccar Point by Sir James Hall. It was the first volume of Lyell's *Principles of Geology* (1830) which the young Darwin took with him on the *Beagle* and which he said opened his eyes to geology, repeatedly referring to it and the two later volumes, which were sent out to him. In his account of the *Beagle* voyage we can empathise with Darwin's struggle to accept the evidence of his eyes, which told him of the great age of the Andes. On his return to England he and Lyell became professional and personal friends until the latter's death.

The Parallel Roads of Glen Roy are a striking feature of the Lochaber landscape. In Darwin's early days explanations ran from the legendary to the scientific. Fresh from the *Beagle* in 1838 he had 'eight good days in Glen Roy', trying to solve the riddle of the Parallel Roads and coming up with an answer (which was, sadly, wrong) based on his South American experience. However, in his defence, it was only in 1840 that Louis Agassiz recognised that these were the shorelines of vanished ice-dammed lakes, while a full explanation only came with Jamieson in 1863. And there are still unresolved puzzling features about the area.

Vestiges of Creation created a sensation when it was published in 1844, partly because of its anonymous authorship. Who was the author?

Why did he (or she) want to remain anonymous? Could it really be Prince Albert, according to the report of a joke made at a Liverpool party?

The unknown author put forward a theory of evolution and challenged fundamental Victorian beliefs. The Unknown's anonymity gave him a kind of protection in that the establishment were slow to respond until they could be sure of their target. Then churchmen and scientists were as one in rejecting its message. The Unknown seemed to be questioning the Biblical account of creation and the special status of Man among the animals. The scientists were unhappy that The Unknown did not appear to be of their number and did not seem to have spent many hours grinding away at minutiae and writing papers crowded with detail. Later editions were aimed at, and popular with, the lower and middle classes – which was perceived as a dangerous fault.

Vestiges of the Natural History of Creation is often seen as a kind of curtain-raiser for Darwin's *Origin of Species*. This is too simple, *Vestiges* was an important book in its own right. When it came out, Darwin had written 200 pages on evolution. This had to be abandoned and it was 15 years before *Origin of Species* further progressed thinking on evolution. Darwin in public was as vigorous as any in condemning The Unknown, although in private he expressed some sympathy for his situation. In his study he studied *Vestiges* closely in order to learn how to avoid controversy and still tell the truth simply. Darwin considered the publication of *Vestiges* to have smoothed the way for his *Origin of Species* – its reception certainly made him more cautious when his own time came.

Yet, even after *Origin of Species* entered the field, *Vestiges* continued to maintain its popularity; it was only about 1900 that Darwin's great work finally overtook *Vestiges* in the race for sales. Victorian society in the second half of the 19th century was very fortunate in having available parallel justifications for evolution, the classic scientific text of the heroic Darwin, and the readable *Vestiges* by 'a provincial popular author'.

Robert Chambers, who was officially named as the author after his death, was a grandchild of the Scottish Enlightenment and I will examine his influence, negative as well as positive, on Darwin, at a turning point in his career.

The Plinian Society of Edinburgh University operated from 1823 to 1841. In 1826 the Secretary was Dr Robert Grant (1793–1874), later first Professor of Zoology in University College, London. All commentators agree with Darwin on the importance of Grant and the Society for his development. A controversial paper was read to the society on 21 November 1826 by William Browne. As was his wont, for many years Darwin brooded on the subject, engaging in correspondence and collecting material. He thought of giving it a chapter in *The Descent of Man* (1871), only to find that his mass of information and speculation demanded a book of its own.

The Expression of the Emotions in Man and Animals was published in 1872 and is a very odd book indeed, quite unlike anything else Darwin wrote. He claimed that booksellers had subscribed to 5267 copies on the day of publication, making it his first-day bestseller.

Patrick Geddes (1854–1932) was an Eminent Victorian in his own right, rating an entry of 358 words in the *Who's Who* of 1930. Twice nominated for a knighthood, he received the accolade a mere 52 days before his death. Born in fairly modest circumstances, he made an unconventional way to eminence as 'Biologist, Town Planner, Re-educator, Peace-warrior'. Taking Geddes as a sample, the question is asked: 'How did a young man from a very modest background in a small provincial city, with the sketchiest of qualifications, break into the upper echelons of the scientific society of his time?' Darwin influenced him in three ways and this makes an interesting case study of the effect of 'old Father Darwin' on the next generation.

Geddes was a compulsive educator and a prolific writer, although by no means an easy read. Geddes repaid his debt to Darwin by disseminating and interpreting for the next generation the contributions to knowledge and understanding of 'the greatest Naturalist of the age.' The Geddes approach is one of critical awareness rather than blind hero-worship and in it can be traced the evolution of ideas on evolution after Darwin.

Hutton's 'We find no vestige of a beginning, no prospect of an end' – was an uncomfortable thought which many, in his time and later, have chosen to misunderstand and which some have still not had the courage to accept. That natural selection is the main driver of evolution is the conclusion of observation and reason, but it is a chilling and uncomfortable message for many and it is understandable that they seek comfort in alternative explanations.

For me, it is extremely worrying to hear that, in the United States, the world's richest nation, stuffed full with clever and innovative people, over half the population say that they believe absolutely in the Biblical account of creation, that the Earth and everything in it was created in six days, that that was the end of it, except for the creation of Man, who was created specially in God's image. Other clever and innovative people have brought forward the theory of 'Intelligent Design', that there is a 'higher power' for the complexities of life.

The Biblical account of creation, and of the subsequent Flood, are beautiful and logical narratives. There is another little Biblical narrative worthy of some attention. A rich young man asked Jesus: 'What shall I do to inherit eternal life?' After some discussion he received the answer: 'Sell all that thou hast, and distribute unto the poor, and thou shalt have treasure in heaven.' And when the young man 'heard this he was very sorrowful, for he was very rich.'

When we see scores of fundamentalists carrying out the actions demanded by Scripture we may begin to give some serious attention to their words anent Creation.

Fortunately, the churches – who gave Chambers and Darwin such a hard time in the 19th century – have used the Darwin bicentenary to redefine their relationship with evolutionary thought. In September 2008 the Church of England conceded that it had been 'over-defensive and over-emotional' in dismissing Darwin's ideas. In a statement the Church said: 'Charles Darwin: 200 years from your birth, the Church of England owes you an apology for misunderstanding you', comparing the situation to the mistakes made in the 17th century in doubting Galileo's astronomy.

The headline in *The Times* of 11 February 2009 read: 'Vatican buries the hatchet with Charles Darwin'. Archbishop Gianfranco Ravasi declared that Darwin's theory of evolution was compatible with Christian faith and could even be traced to St Augustine and St Thomas Aquinas: 'In fact, what we mean by evolution is the world as created by God.' At a papal-backed Darwin conference in March it had been intended to ban Intelligent Design. Instead, it was given a marginal slot as a 'cultural phenomenon' rather than a scientific or theological issue.

Much is usually made of the influence on Darwin of 'the Cambridge set', and some of this will emerge as we proceed further. Darwin was not surrounded by Scots, but some of the most significant influences came from his Edinburgh days and from the wandering Scots he came across at crucial points in his career, several of whom had made the transition to the national scientific community centred on London.

When we aggregate the experiences and influences of these Scots, most of them children or grandchildren of the Enlightenment, on Darwin, we are struck by the range and diversity of their thinking, but we are also struck by the range and diversity of his achievement.

For whatever reason, Darwin undervalued the time spent in Edinburgh as a student, yet he owed much to Hutton, Chambers and others of similar background.

As already suggested, Darwin did not burst, perfectly formed, from the brow of some goddess. The high level of Scottish scientific thought in Darwin's time had its influence on the great man.

He made mistakes and false starts, but he had something to teach us – not only about science – but in how to cope with frustration and adversity.

CHAPTER TWO

Darwin and the
Vestiges of Creation

ONE OF MY favourite images is conjured up by a piece of music by Erik Satie (1866–1925), one of the *avant-garde* of the 1920s, known as *Les Six*. His *Gymnopédie No 2* became very popular among the young in the 1960s when its long, gentle, flowing phrases seemed to sum up the dreamier side of that cultural revolution. On paper it looks very easy, even dull, but on my instrument, the clarinet, its long, long phrases twisting and turning gently for many, many bars must be taken without a breath, which is, of course, impossible.

Gymnopédie is meant to represent the statue of a beautiful young man on a plinth which rotates very slowly, while a powerful light throws up subtleties of light and shade, which alter as he slowly turns.

For Darwin and the *Vestiges of the Natural History of Creation*, what is to be placed on the plinth and illuminated? Fairly recently the BBC ran a very interesting series seeking to find out who was the Greatest Briton of all time? A short leet of 10 or 12 was decided, and then an advocate for each candidate gave a short justification for the audience to cast their votes for him or her. The candidates were kings and queens, military and naval leaders, politicians and the like. Isambard Kingdom Brunel made the short leet as a man of peace who created mighty works of great benefit to society. The winner, by popular acclaim, had to be Winston Churchill who had, in the span of five short years, taken a defeated and dispirited country, united it and led it to destroy one of the vilest regimes in history. Running him close, however, was another man of peace, who shunned publicity and was happiest when he was among his barnacles, his pigeons or his earthworms. Even the great British public recognised that in Darwin they had a Great Man who had faced the great questions of life and their meaning and had managed to draw a large section of the population into the consideration of these questions. Darwin was an Eminent Victorian who was too eminent for Lytton Strachey[2], who preferred softer targets like Cardinal Manning and Florence Nightingale.

The book itself could be placed on the pedestal, where it deserves to be. Handsomely got up, the first editions were aimed at: 'the higher classes and for libraries', and caused a sensation. The time was ripe for a sensation. Ideas were whirling around, disturbing ideas about humanity – its origins, its emotions, its beliefs. Traditionalists were enraged at the blasphemous implications of all this excitement. What we would call book groups now had something to get their teeth into. *Vestiges* became a family book, often being given by men to women. The final seal of approval came early in 1845 when Prince Albert read *Vestiges* aloud to the young Victoria – bored by technical monographs and the British Association – each afternoon. *Vestiges* had made science a shared interest among the higher classes and was soon to become available, in cheap editions, to a much larger public, with whom it came to be associated.

There is a danger that we see everything that happened in the 19th century as having been centred on Darwin, with the consequent danger that we see *Vestiges* as being no more than – to change the metaphor – a John the Baptist preparing the way for the Messiah yet to come – Charles Darwin. But James Secord, in 584 pages, has winnowed, ground and sieved every conceivable piece of evidence on the *Extraordinary Publication, Reception and Secret Authorship of Vestiges of the Natural History of Creation* to establish that it is a major work in its own right. In 1844 it was the latest wisdom and not a forerunner of anything else, and we would do well to remember that when we examine it closely.

On the plinth we would normally expect to see the author and to be able to note his characteristics and irregularities. But the book is rare in that its title page bears no author's name; instead, an important medical publisher – John Churchill of London – figures prominently. Part of the appeal of *Vestiges* lay in the mystery of the anonymous author and there was much speculation about his (or her) identity. There was irritation also as reviewers showed uncertainty about which line to take. Only when the true identity began to emerge did the hatchets begin to come out in earnest – and by then it was too late, the book was already a bestseller.

It was only in 1884, in the 12th edition, that it was revealed officially that the author was Robert Chambers, a prolific writer and publisher, who had died in 1871. Chambers referred to himself as 'The Unknown', inviting comparison with Sir Walter Scott, who had been 'The Great Unknown'. He also used 'Ignotus', 'Sir Roger' and 'Mr Balderstone'. Anne Chambers, who rewrote the manuscript so that Chambers' writing would not be recognised, was 'Mrs Balderstone'. (A sharp reader might have noted that Mr and Mrs Balderstone were fictionalised versions of the Chambers in *Chambers Journal*.)

The whole business is clearly very complicated but can, I think, be clarified by going back to Satie's rotating plinth, as if we were in 1844 and coming across the book for the first time, asking a question of each of the subjects, in the following order:

What did *Vestiges* actually say and why did so many find it disturbing? Who was Robert Chambers and why did he try to remain anonymous? What did Darwin think of *Vestiges* and how did it affect his later behaviour?

What did Vestiges *actually say and why did so many find it disturbing?*

Vestiges of the Natural History of Creation begins quite simply, even starkly, with an uncluttered title page, a list of Contents and goes straight into the first chapter – 'The Bodies of Space: Their Arrangements and Formation':

> It is familiar knowledge that the earth which we inhabit is a globe of somewhat less than 8,000 miles in diameter, being one of a series of eleven which revolve at different distances around the sun, and some of which have satellites in like manner revolving around them.

He defines the solar system, defines its size, then, since 'the mind fails to form an exact notion of a portion of space so immense' tells us how long it would take a galloping horse to cover that distance.

The statement oozes knowledge and certainty, demonstrating that we are in the presence of an authority; not an amateur, at the very least an experienced journalist. Yet at the same time he draws us in by suggesting that we are on the same plane as he, and by his use of a homely example. The anonymous author writes easily, almost conversationally; he is an expert and a communicator. The chapter continues with the author setting out his nebular hypothesis of the universe; that stars, planets and moons have all condensed from a gaseous 'Fire-mist'. The next chapter deals with the: 'Constituent Materials of the Earth, and of the other Bodies of Space'. Chapter 4 is: 'Commencement of Organic Life – Sea Plants, Corals, etc'. Chapter 8 is: 'Era of the Oolite – Commencement of Mammalia'. There is a progression summarised here, a progression we can recognise from another source.

In the first chapter of Genesis a progression is also described. On the first day Day and Night were created.

On the second day God made the firmament. On page 20 of *Vestiges* The Unknown begins to describe the composition of the firmament – he uses that word.

On the third day God said: 'let the dry land appear' and 'Let the earth bring forth grass.' Chapter 6 of *Vestiges* is: 'Secondary Rocks – Era of the Carboniferous Formation – Land formed – Commencement of Land Plants'.

The fifth day saw the creation of fishes and birds. In *Vestiges* Chapter 5 is: 'Era of the Old Red Sandstone – Fishes abundant'. while Chapter 7 is: 'Era of the New Red Sandstone – Terrestrial Zoology commences with Reptiles – First traces of Birds'.

On the sixth day God created the land animals: 'and God saw that it was good.' Then, and this is important, He made man in His own image and let him 'have dominion over' the other forms of life. In *Vestiges* Chapter 8 is: 'Era of the Oolite – Commencement of Mammalia', while mammals become abundant in Chapter 10. The 'superiority' of man is demonstrated by his being dealt with in four chapters, starting in the: 'Era of the Superficial Formations – Commencement of present Species' and going on through 'General Considerations respecting the Origin of the Animated Tribes' to 'Particular Considerations respecting the Origin of the Animated Tribes' and 'Early History of Mankind'.

'Thus the heavens and the earth were finished' and He 'rested on the seventh day from all His work which He had done.' Chapter 18 of *Vestiges* is reflective. 'Purpose and General Condition of the Animated Creation' is followed by 'Note Conclusory'.

There is a clear parallelism between creation, as described in Genesis, and transmutation, as described in *Vestiges of Creation*. ('Evolution' in the Darwinian sense did not come into use till the 1870s). In effect, the anonymous author of *Vestiges* had made creation itself the subject of a natural history. Indeed *The Natural History of Creation* was the initial choice of title, only to be abandoned as too aggressive and likely to rouse adverse criticism. Fossils – and fossils were the 'vestiges of creation' – for example, showed a progression from simple to more complex organisms, with Man the latest arrival at the top of creation. Even Man showed a progression from Negro to Malayan, to the aboriginal American, to the Mongolian, to the Caucasian. These 'varieties', however, according to the author: 'may have had one origin' – too radical a thought for some, like Louis Agassiz, in later years.

The book makes much of 'natural law', which suggests that God did not interact after the original creation, continually intervening with miracles, having done all that was necessary for it to work. Opponents saw this as a denial of Christianity, in which the central miracle is that God sent His son to save the world.

The narrative was, however, not just an expansion of the Biblical account, it differed from it in some other respects. These were to become areas of contention. Genesis emphasised the differences between Man and other species: he was a separate – the final – creation, he was superior to the other animals, he was made in God's image. God was able to rest on the seventh day because His work was complete and perfect; therefore the number of species could not increase, neither could they change. However, the fossil record (the 'vestiges of creation') showed that many forms of life had flourished at various periods, only to become extinct. How could this be if God's creation was perfect?

The Bible's account of creation is one page of wonderful description, with a beginning, a middle and an end and an apparently simple message. The author of *Vestiges* takes 390 pages to deliver his message, taking each geological period in turn, explaining and giving examples, piling one piece of evidence on top of another. The book, as the anonymous author wrote, was 'Composed in solitude and almost without the cognisance of a single human being.' In a science as new as geology then was, one can make a lot of mistakes or wrong observations in 390 pages and the author was very conscious that he was leaving himself open to attack.

The author's anxiety was shown in another way. 150 copies of the first edition (out of 1,000 printed) were sent to leading libraries, periodicals and potentially interested individuals, in order to soften them up and to generate positive feedback. As a result of this campaign, or intrinsic merit, or its reasonable price – 7/6 (37.5p) for 390 pages – the book sold well and continued to sell well. A third edition of 1,500 copies was bought up by the book trade on the day of publication. The book had to be revised regularly and in the years to 1860 went through 11 editions and sold 23,350 copies. Differences in the style, size and binding of the various editions ensured that they gained entry to the social ladder at different points.

Originally, the author's elegant prose ('it reads like a novel' – not a recommendation for some!) was enough to take the reader through the text, but the 10th and 11th editions were illustrated (the illustrator's fee was £75). Its accessibility – to its critics its most dangerous feature – ensured its success even after the publication of *Origin of Species* in 1859. Indeed it was as late as 1890 before *Origin of Species* overtook *Vestiges* in terms of total sales.

Views for and against *Vestiges* were aired in several semi-formal contexts. The Murchisons, in the spring of 1845, held a series of great soirées as part of their campaign to become Sir Roderick and Lady Murchison – ideal occasions for consideration of *Vestiges*. The learned London societies held 'conversations' around the book's issues without mentioning it by name. Even women entered into the debate, which, according to James Secord in *Victorian Sensation*, 'offered wonderful opportunities for displaying conversational skill.' *Punch,* always sensitive to social change, printed jokes, puns and cartoons.

Vestiges could be attacked on various grounds. It was a big book for one man to write unaided (which he did), science was changing rapidly and some of the material was recycled from *Chambers Edinburgh Journal.* The London geologists were soon hard at work, comparing notes and sending letters thick and fast. Errors in *Vestiges* were checked against those in Chambers' other works. The author was repeatedly attacked on his facts, as this was safe and uncontroversial. For example, he adopted a classification of the organic world based on a hierarchy of clustered groups of five. This was dropped for the third edition, to be replaced by a system of genetic lines, with no single chain of being.

It is a mistake to judge 'big books' like *Vestiges, Principles of Geology* and *Origin of Species* by the first editions alone. They were 'serial publications' – interactive in the modern sense – in that each of the many new editions took account of reviews and comments from experts and the reading public and from new knowledge. (For example, see the small print of the Third Edition of *Origin of Species* on the Frontispiece). There is an intellectual satisfaction in realising that these big books about evolution were themselves undergoing an evolutionary process and – thinking of 'the survival of the fittest' – that *Vestiges* was to die out while *Origin of Species* was to prosper.

Explanations: A Sequel to 'Vestiges of the Natural History of Creation' by The Author of that Work was produced by the same anonymous author and published by the same circuitous route in late 1845. With the same paper, page size, type and binding as *Vestiges,* in 209 pages it set the record straight in many respects.

Principles, in other words, religion, were trickier to handle. There was much controversy and vilification – the author was described as: 'credulous, superficial, sceptical, imaginative, childlike, crazed, hypothetical, and fantastical.' The churches, particularly the Church of England and the recently-formed Free Church in Scotland, were most upset. Many scientists were negative. Lyell, whom we shall meet later:

> ...condemned the book on the basis of reports from other geologists without even reading the copy the author had sent him. (*Liverpool Journal*, 2 February 1845)

The author clearly came from the rational Scottish Enlightenment background of Hutton, Playfair and Lyell himself. Ranged against him were the Cambridge establishment of Buckland, Sedgwick and Henslow, Darwin's mentors at Cambridge and in later life. All three were first-class geologists with a fine record at the micro level, well able to recognise and analyse rocks, to identify faults and folds, to find and reconstruct past environments from fossils – those 'vestiges of creation'. But they were to prove to have major shortcomings at the macro level, in conceptualising the big picture of how all these elements fitted together. Sedgwick's reaction to *Vestiges* is worthy of study.

The Reverend Adam Sedgwick (1785–1873) in 1844 was a force in the land, a champion of science and faith. Friends looked to him to fight against the infidelity of *Vestiges*. He procrastinated. He did not read *Vestiges* carefully for several months. Then he began to see his reluctance as a lack of moral courage and agreed to review the book for the *Edinburgh Review*. Why the volte-face? It is suggested that he had worked out, from internal evidence, that the author was a woman and then he was told she was Ada, Countess of Lovelace (Lord Byron's only legitimate daughter), rich and with a lively mind: 'a right true blue.'

Now Sedgwick knew his enemy and could write his review. As he told Lyell:

> I cannot but think the work is from a woman's pen, it is so well dressed, and so graceful in its externals...the reading, though extensive, is very shallow, and the author perpetually...leaps to a conclusion, as if the toilsome way up the hill of Truth were to be passed over with the light skip of an opera-dancer.

Although Sedgwick mounted a fierce, if polite, argument against the authority of the supposed author; it could have been used, slightly modified, against the actual author. Sedgwick presented himself as a leading man of science, speaking on behalf of an imagined united scientific community. Actual scientific discovery involved 'enormous and continued labour' – what we would now call 'time on task' – for which women were unsuited:

> We know, by long experience, that the ascent up the hill of science is rugged and thorny, and ill-fitted for the drapery of a petticoat, and ways must be passed over which are toilsome to the body, and sometimes loathsome to the senses.

No doubt the rigours of such an ascent would also have been beyond a professional writer on scientific topics. There was a huge divide in nature between man and beast, said Sedgwick. God suspended natural law from time to time and created new species of plants and animals as necessary: 'by the repeated operation of creative power.' The author of *Vestiges* scotched the notion that subsequent creations might have taken place:

> How can we suppose that the august Being who brought all these countless worlds into form by the simple establishment of a natural principle flowing from his mind, was to interfere personally and specially on every occasion when a new shell-fish or reptile was to be ushered into existence on one of these worlds? Surely this idea is too ridiculous to be for a moment entertained.

We can be spared the detail of the 85 page article which appeared in the *Edinburgh Review* of July 1845. Such reviews were anonymous but Sedgwick made it his business to ensure that his authorship was widely recognised. While the aggressive tone did not go down well in many drawing rooms, a substantial body of scientists and churchmen took comfort in Sedgwick. As we shall see, Sedgwick had great influence on Darwin who, at the very least, had to think very carefully about what he was going to say in his presence.

Chambers, as Chambers and not as the author of *Vestiges,* came to the British Association meeting at Oxford in 1847 to speak on ancient beaches. Sir Archibald Geikie reminisced, in 1895, that Chambers:

> pushed his conclusions to a most unwarrantable length, and got roughly handled on account of it by Buckland, Sedgwick, Murchison and Lyell. The last told me afterwards that he did so purposely that C. might see that reasonings in the style of the author of the *Vestiges* would not be tolerated among scientific men.

On the Sunday, Bishop Wilberforce ('Soapy Sam' as he was later to be known, when he foolishly took on Huxley) preached on the wrong way to do science, at the 'half-learned'. The main themes of *Vestiges* were taken apart. The scholars loved it. The coalition of gentlemen and clergy objected to sloppy science coming from a magazine publisher and were crushing him in consequence. Chambers had no alternative but to fume in his pew, denouncing to himself these 'dogs of clergy' who were attempting to stifle progressive opinion.

For a contemporary verdict on *Vestiges of the Natural History of Creation* I turn to Desmond and Moore, joint-authors of two major works on Darwin – *Darwin* (1991) and *Darwin's Sacred Cause* (2009). Excellent though they are, they suffer from the same fault. In their efforts to boost Darwin and his reputation they tend to denigrate others around him. This is what they say about Chambers and *Vestiges:*

> The book, an anonymous potboiler, argued that continual miraculous tinkerings with species were unnecessary.

> This evolutionary potboiler of medical-fringe ideas made the succession of fossil animals (the 'vestiges') tell a story about life's hereditary bloodline.

...a hackwork, and flawed.

...a racy, unreferenced pot-boiler like *Vestiges*.

...the flighty *Vestiges* pandering to the lowest taste.

[Darwin] was still afraid of a hack queering his pitch.

Vestiges was attacked on two grounds which were, in fact, its greatest strength.

It was attacked because the unknown author had tried too much, had tried to write a big book on the biggest of subjects, and was not up to it. Perhaps not, but it had opened the eyes of a generation and had generated purposeful debate, which lasted for at least the 15 years before the publication of the next building block in the structure of human self-knowledge – *The Origin of Species*.

The writer was not a leading man of science, had not devoted 'enormous and continued labour' to the task. He had no authority. Yet what were the Cambridge divines and other self-styled men of science doing? Their income came from the University and the Church; were they any more professional men of science than the journalist? Dealing with minutiae, too stupid, too blinkered or too cowardly, they were content to leave the consideration of the biggest issues to 'a hack'.

Who was Robert Chambers and why did he try to remain anonymous?

Peebles is a small town in the Scottish Borders, 23 miles south of the General Post Office in Edinburgh. On the Tweed, it was a Royal Burgh, the county town and an early centre for textile production. Henry Cockburn, in *Memorials of his Time*, described 'The Radical War' of 1820, when 'Edinburgh was as quiet as the grave, or even as Peebles.' The father of Robert Chambers was the manager of a large network of hand-loom weavers but was a casualty of the change to the factory system. After the education of his sons at the local school the family moved to Edinburgh in order to retrieve the family fortunes.

William Chambers (1800–83) was the older son and was apprenticed to a bookseller. He went on to printing, then publishing and writing books. He was an innovator in revolutionising the production of books and in developing and marketing new styles of publication, particularly reference books and periodicals. *Chambers Edinburgh Journal* attained a circulation of 80,000. Started in 1832, it ran until 1956. (In the context of authorial anonymity, it is relevant to note that the first British detective story – by 'Waters' – appeared in *Chambers Edinburgh Journal* in July 1849). *Chambers Encyclopaedia* we will encounter later. First published in 1859–68, it was a 'user-friendly' rival to the *Encyclopaedia Britannica*.

With his early struggles and lifelong interest in education and self-improvement it is not surprising to find that his two terms as Lord Provost of Edinburgh were as energetic as his business life. An Improvement Act of 1867 led to the reconstruction of great swathes of the Old Town. The high point was Chambers Street (c.1870), a great processional way with a splendid statue of Chambers, on a very substantial plinth, looking towards the Border hills and with grandiose institutions on either side. Fifty years ago, the south side was made up of the Old Quad of Edinburgh University, the Royal Scottish Museum and a Heriot Trust school (demolished for the National Museum of Scotland). The north side had The Edinburgh Dental Hospital and School, Heriot-Watt College and other university buildings. At a later date Chambers proposed and carried out, largely at his own expense, the restoration of the Cathedral Church of St Giles. To his native town he presented a museum, library and art gallery. This 'Chambers' Institution' still has a valuable role in the community life of Peebles.

Robert Chambers (1802–71) at an early age 'gave evidence of unusual literary taste and ability,' but poverty meant that his start in life was as a bookstall-keeper on Leith Walk, hardly the most select street in Edinburgh. In reminiscent mood in later life Chambers said:

> Books, not playthings, filled my hands in childhood. At twelve I was deep, not only in poetry and fiction, but encyclopedias.

He joined his brother as a partner in W. & R. Chambers, which was a successful enterprise for more than 150 years. The brothers were a good working partnership, otherwise they lived separate lives. Robert was a man of prodigious energy; his output was enormous, although very variable and often quite ephemeral.

Parallels are often drawn between Walter Scott and Robert Chambers. Both were Borderers, in a sense. Scott came from a Border family, travelled round the Borders collecting material for the *Minstrelsy of the Scottish Border* and built for himself a splendid second home at Abbotsford. Chambers spent his first few years in the Borders before moving to Edinburgh, where both parties spent the bulk of their working lives. His *Traditions of Edinburgh, The Popular Rhymes of Scotland* and several works on Burns did for the rest of Scotland what Scott had done for his own territory. Chambers was a keen golfer and, to test his veracity, I thought it a good idea to look at his essay on 'John Paterson, the Golfer'.

In the Canongate is a block of flats on the site of Golfer's Land, with a plaque explaining how John Paterson had bought the property from his winnings when he partnered James VII and II against two English noblemen. His motto, 'Far and Sure', has become the motto of many golf clubs around the world. Chambers' *Traditions of Edinburgh* has an engraving of the original Golfer's Land and tells the story through citing earlier writers. He concludes, however: 'It must be admitted there is some uncertainty about this tale', and gives reasons for his doubts, only to concede:

> The tradition, nevertheless, seems too curious to be entirely over-looked, and the reader may therefore take it at its worth.

At the age of 22, Chambers is serving notice that he is prepared to think for himself and not meekly recycle the views of others.

A sad little exhibit in Lady Stair's House ('The Writers' Museum') is the small rocking horse made for the young Walter Scott, with the supports on either side at different levels to cope with his crippled leg. Scott's disability ruled him out of manly pursuits yet he turned it to good effect by constructing a vicariously adventurous world of the imagination. Chambers had the misfortune to be born with six fingers and toes on each hand and foot. This must surely have affected his attitudes and the attitudes of others. Certainly, when his daughter proved to have been born with the same defect he was able to joke: 'We are manifesting a tendency to return to the reptilian type' but had no hesitation in having the surplus digits removed. Darwin, also, went through agonies of indecision when contemplating marriage to his first cousin and, given some of the outcomes of the match, he may have been right to do so.

Both Scott and Chambers took refuge in anonymity. Scott was a senior law officer, Sheriff of Selkirk and a gentleman; writing novels should have been beneath him and from 1815 the title pages of his books said they were by 'The Author of *Waverley*'. Although the identity of 'The Great Unknown' was at least guessed at much earlier, it was only on 23 February 1827 at the Theatrical Fund Dinner, that Scott publicly confessed to the authorship of the Waverley Novels: 'The joke had lasted long enough and I was tired of it.'

The author of *Traditions of Edinburgh*, when it came to *Vestiges*, followed in the footsteps of 'The Author of Waverley' by keeping his identity secret – although he acknowledged the similarity of circumstance by referring to himself as 'The Unknown'. He knew that *Vestiges* would ruffle feathers and played safe.

Chambers was much influenced by Scott, who liked him: 'in part because he understood I was from Tweedside.' Chambers contrived to attract Scott's attention and when George IV visited Edinburgh was commissioned to write the address of the Royal Society of Edinburgh to His Majesty – for which he was 'handsomely paid'. Scott was astonished as to 'where the boy got all the information' for the *Traditions* – an astounding reaction from one so erudite as Scott.

Scott called on Chambers one day – which overwhelmed him: 'for Sir Walter Scott was almost an object of worship for me.' Sir Walter sent him pages of reminiscences and 'whole sheets of his recollections, with appropriate explanations.'

Twice Chambers has a significant mention in Scott's *Journal*. On 15 November 1827:

> Met with Chambers and complimented him about his making a clever book of the 1745 for Constable's *Miscellany*. It is really a lively work and must have a good sale. I suppose old Fraud and Suet (Constable the publisher) fop-doodled him out of the money, poor lad.

No-one knew better than Scott the dangers of overwork. His comment of 15 February 1829 is therefore worth noting:

> I wrought today but not much – rather dawdled and took to reading Chambers' *Beauties of Scotland* which would be admirable if they were more accurate. He is a clever young fellow but hurts himself by too much haste.

The reputation for industry was used, years later, as a defence when, as reported in *Victorian Sensation*, Chambers was challenged at his own dinner table, when the conversation turned to *Vestiges*. A lady blurted out: 'Do you know, Mr Chambers, some people say you wrote that book.' Continuing to carve the lamb, Chambers replied: 'I wonder how people can suppose I ever had time to write such a book.'

It is not necessary to list Chambers' output as author, contributor and editor, which was prodigious. He had some reputation as a scientific geologist and did not merely sit in his study recycling 'other men's flowers'; he carried out his own investigations in the field. (*Tracings of the North of Europe* – 1851 – and *Tracings in Iceland and the Faroe Islands* – 1856 – were other results.) Four years after the anonymous publication of *Vestiges of Creation,* he paid two visits to Glen Roy, where Darwin had worked in 1838. (Chambers, in the absence of a reliable map, employed an engineer with a spirit level, but there was some doubt about his datum level and exactly where on the shelving beaches heights were being recorded).

Darwin wrote Chambers a long letter of advice, in which he asked if he (Darwin) might call on him, and in another letter he maintained that features of the topography of Glen Roy convinced him that his marine theory was correct. (This may have been the meeting immediately after which Chambers sent Darwin a copy of *Vestiges*.)

The result was *Ancient Sea Margins*, which came out in 1848, the title page proudly proclaiming that Robert Chambers was a Fellow of the Royal Society of Edinburgh. Here we have a plot worthy of a 19th century comic opera. Darwin writes a paper that is contradicted by the world's leading naturalist. An unknown writer publishes a book which turns conventional wisdom upside down. Darwin finds this difficult to take but is reassured when a leading geologist publishes a book in his support. Unknown to Darwin the cause of his concern and his benefactor are one and the same person.

Robert Chambers lived with this kind of situation for many years. At times he must have enjoyed the ambiguity and the intrigue. Rather cleverly, at one period he maintained a pew in each of two churches, thereby ensuring that his movements on the Sabbath could not be closely scrutinised. At other times he must have found secrecy and subterfuge irritating and frustrating. Why the anonymity?

Anonymity of authorship was not unusual in the 19th century. It was perfectly respectable for a gentleman to write a treatise on the cultivation of flax, or the best planting mix for poor land, but not to be responsible for what the present-day bookseller in the High Street of Peebles displays as 'paper-backed novels.' Just as the author's name may sell a title, if the book flops the author may flop with it.

A prolific author may flood the market by producing too many similar books in quick succession. In the late 19th century William Sharp (1855–1905) wrote more than 20 books of poetry and literary biography under his own name and another twelve or so in the Celtic Revival style as 'Fiona MacLeod'. Titles such as *Mountain Lovers, The Sin-Eater and Other Tales* and *The Divine Adventure* suggest why. He may have learned from Chambers how to preserve his dual identity; he dictated his text to his sister, whose handwriting would be passed off as Fiona's.

In the 20th century, John Creasey (1908–73) was responsible for some 560 'paper-backed novels' in 40 years, written under 22 pseudonyms.

Vestiges of Creation might have been written by a woman. Misdirection was common among women writers. Charlotte Brontë started off as 'Currer Bell'. One looks in vain on the library shelves for Marian Evans, who never gave up the pseudonym of George Eliot. *Pride and Prejudice* was described in the *Morning Post* as: 'a novel by a Lady, the author of *Sense and Sensibility*.' Was there a woman with a brain so large that she could astonish the world with such a searching work as *Vestiges*? Ada, Lady Lovelace was such a one, and before *Vestiges* appeared, had already published anonymously.

Robert Chambers had two reasons for choosing anonymity. One was quite normal for the time. *Vestiges* was a new kind of venture and he, and the firm of W. & R. Chambers, would not risk the possibility of failure. In the event, anonymity ensured that the book was noticed and reviewed. And because the book was anonymous it tended to be reviewed on its merits and not as the work of an 'inexperienced bungler'.

As we have seen, Chambers need not have worried on this score, the work was a success from the outset, assured by the whiff of mystery about the authorship.

Chambers knew that *Vestiges* was going to cause trouble. In the 1830s and 1840s:

He had little interest in religion, and references to divine design in the *Journal* and *Vestiges* were largely strategic.

'With its polite exterior, devout language, and decorous prose,' Chambers hoped to defuse criticism of his lack of a strong personal faith, and placate those who thought he was setting aside the Scriptures. In his 'Note Conclusory' he stressed that religious critics would find:

Nothing in it of a worse character than geology when you consider its inconsistency with the Mosaic record,

and concluded:

Thus we give, as is meet, a respectful reception to what is revealed through the medium of nature, at the same time that we fully reserve our reverence for all we have been accustomed to hold sacred, not one tittle of which it may ultimately be found necessary to alter.

Chambers may not have been successful in pulling the wool over the eyes of his critics. Sir John Cam Hobhouse, in his diary, wrote:

In spite of the allusions to the creative will of God the cosmogony is atheistic – at least the introduction of an author of all things seems very like a formality for the sake of saving appearances – it is not a necessary part of the scheme.

Remaining anonymous was a shield against a violent and abusive controversy. You can't have an argument *ad hominem* if you don't know who the *hominem* is. When asked by his son-in-law many years later:

why his greatest book was shrouded in impenetrable mystery (Chambers) pointed to his house, in which he had 11 children, and then slowly added, 'I have 11 reasons.'

The exiled Charles X of France spent some time in the Sanctuary of Holyroodhouse. Among his followers was one Edouarts, who supplemented his meagre wages by producing a stream of silhouettes of the local notabilities and stayed on as an observer of the Edinburgh scene. One charming silhouette shows Anne Chambers playing the harp, surrounded by eight of her children. When we observe this, can we be surprised at

Chambers' reluctance to put them in the spotlight of public opinion? We would also ask: If the tone-deaf Darwin was soothed and inspired (as some say) in the evenings by Emma Darwin on the piano, how would the *Vestiges* have been influenced by the lovely domestic scene of the talented Mrs Chambers with her arpeggios, surrounded by her intently reading brood?

The details of publishing *Vestiges* read like a tale of espionage. First, Chambers wrote the text. In case his handwriting was recognised his wife copied the entire manuscript. (She did the same with the changes to the various editions and with most of the incoming correspondence.) The text was then passed on to Alexander Ireland, a Manchester journalist, who acted as the link between Edinburgh and London. The publisher was the reputable John Churchill, who published the *Lancet* and had stood up to vicious attacks on another author in the same field. The new postal system of 1837 made it possible for amendments, proofs and the like to be moved back and forward along the chain speedily and reliably.

Speculation about the identity of the author was a favourite parlour game for years, until a disgruntled geologist/writer began a leak at the time of the tenth edition in 1853. In 1844 Victorian society was settling down to respectability after the duelling and gambling of the Regency. (The last duel in Scotland was fought in 1822 in Fife – convenient for flight to the Continent). The fate of few loyal tenants of estates were now to hang on the turn of a card – at least until the Prince of Wales once more made hedonism fashionable. I have come across no evidence to suggest that bets were placed or that there was a Great Vestiges Handicap, but it is tempting to think that someone at the time drew up a card of 'runners and riders' for easy reference, something like this.

The Fillies

Harriet Martineau – writer, philosopher, feminist. Close to Erasmus, Charles Darwin's older brother.

Ada Lovelace – romantic scientist, networked with half the runners.

Catherine Crowe – novelist, spiritualist, covered for Chambers.

Anne Chambers – could go the distance, dark horse.

Carrying Top Weight

Sir Richard Rawlinson Vyvyan – good form, early favourite.
Lord Lovelace – keen supporter of *Vestiges*.
Lord Thurlow – keen supporter of *Vestiges*.
Lord Brougham – founded *Edinburgh Review*, Lord Chancellor.
Sir Charles Bunbury – Lyell's brother-in-law, keen beginner.
Edward Bunbury – Whig brother of above. Form unknown.
Andrew Crosse – country squire, strong on insects.

Great Brains

Charles Lyell – author of *Principles of Geology*.
George Combe – Scots phrenologist, covered for Chambers.
Charles Babbage – inventor of a calculating machine.
William Makepeace Thackeray – author of *Vanity Fair*.

Outsiders

William Carpenter – physiologist, tutored Lovelaces, praised *Vestiges*.
John Pringle Nichol – astronomer, Scot.
David Page – disgruntled geologist/writer for W. & R. Chambers, reviewed
    Vestiges 1844, accused by *Dundee, Perth & Cupar Advertiser* 1854.
Alexander Bain – moral philosopher, yet another Scot.
Hewett Watson – botanist, ecologist, Edinburgh graduate.
William Hodgson – principal of Mechanics' Institution, Liverpool.
Prince Albert – report of a joke made at a Liverpool party.
Edward Forbes – up-and-coming philosophical naturalist. (Edinburgh.)
Robert Chambers – 'a provincial popular author'.
Robert Chambers, Professor Nichol and a prominent member of the
    Manchester Literary and Philosophical Society – entered in 1859.[3]
Charles Darwin – 'invalid geologist and author of a round-the-world
    travel book.'

What did Darwin think of Vestiges and how did it affect his later behaviour?

In October 1838 the 'invalid geologist and author of a round-the-world travel book' picked up the sixth edition of Thomas Malthus's *Essay on the Principle of Population* which described how population was out-stripping food supply and the weak and improvident were succumbing in the struggle for available resources. Transferring this thinking to the natural world, it occurred to Darwin that, in circumstances like these, favourable variations would tend to be preserved and unfavourable destroyed, resulting in the formation of new species. He began to work on this theory, but not to publish for fear of criticism. By June 1842 he had a brief resumé of 35 pages and by the summer of 1844 230 pages. Then came the publication of *Vestiges*. The Unknown had stolen Darwin's clothes. Darwin had been scooped.

Darwin never bought a copy of *Vestiges*. It was on his list to buy but was sold out when he got to London. He came by his copy of the sixth 'gentleman's' edition in 1847 in an interesting way. Having had a meeting with Robert Chambers on the subject of Glen Roy, a complimentary copy was sent by the post to his home, and this he proceeded to mark up. This must have confirmed, for Darwin, Chambers' authorship. By sending Darwin the book Chambers was paying him the compliment that he was to be trusted to share the secret of authorship.

This is not to say that Darwin was ignorant of *Vestiges* till 1847. James Secord suggests: 'He read the new work in the bustling, flea-infested British Museum library.' He had found the reviews almost as important as the book. He missed 'Soapy Sam's' sermon at the British Association meeting at Oxford in 1847 but attended for the rest of the week, when he slated The Unknown's 'poverty of intellect' and dismissed the book as a 'literary curiosity.' When he learned that he had been named as the possible author he said he was: 'much flattered and unflattered' by the attribution of such a 'strange unphilosophical, but capitally written book.' To Hooker he wrote that the author's 'writing and arrangement are certainly admirable, but his geology strikes me as bad, and his zoology far worse.'

Darwin could be equivocal in his judgment. On the one hand the book had done harm by muddying the waters and spreading half-baked knowledge. On the other, by stirring up controversy, it had exposed the nature of the opposition to transmutation, or evolution, allowing Darwin, in turn, to get his retaliation in first. Sedgwick attacked The Unknown, who replied moderately in *Explanations: A Sequel to the 'Vestiges'*. Darwin's reaction was to say that 'Mr Vestiges' 'spirit...ought to shame Sedgwick.'

Huxley hated *Vestiges* and pronounced accordingly – only to have qualms later. Darwin thought he had overdone it:

> I must think that such a book, if it does no other good, spreads the taste for Natural Science. But I am perhaps no fair judge, for I am almost as unorthodox about species as the *Vestiges* though I hope not quite so unphilosophical.

> I think he is too severe – you may say 'birds of a feather flock together' and therefore I sympathise with the author.

Although critics questioned The Unknown's religious credentials Chambers demonstrated that he could turn the other cheek. Huxley was an applicant for the chair in Natural History at Edinburgh in 1854. He was apprehensive that his review of *Vestiges* would be thrown back in his face, instead Chambers invited him to stay at Number 1 Doune Terrace. What must Huxley have been thinking as he marched up to the front door of 1 Doune Terrace for the first time? The situation was intriguing. Chambers knew he was The Unknown, while Huxley suspected he was, but dared not suggest it. What did they discuss at breakfast over the eggs and devilled kidneys? Golf? But that would bring up *Ancient Sea Margins* and that awful day at Oxford. Or the weather? But the East Coast haar might have been rolling in from the Firth of Forth, reminding them again of *Ancient Sea Margins*. Chambers, I am sure, enjoyed the intrigue and the sight of 'Darwin's bulldog' wriggling in his discomfiture.

FIG 1: No 1 Doune Terrace, Edinburgh

However, while Darwin was publicly denigrating *Vestiges,* he was at the same time studying it closely. Darwin used *Vestiges* as a means of deciding how his own theory should be presented. He did not read *Vestiges* as a continuous narrative or a 'good read'; he saw it as an unsatisfactory version of what he himself might have written and sought to learn how he could make his own version both more accurate and less controversial. Thus he quickly skimmed great chunks which had stirred the general reader, while carefully noting and condemning its weakest features.

In the Introduction to *On the Origin of Species* Darwin took *Vestiges* to task:

> The author of the *Vestiges of Creation* would, I presume, say that, after a certain unknown number of generations, some bird had given birth to a woodpecker, and some plant to the mistletoe, and that these had been produced perfect as we now see them; but this assumption seems to me to be no explanation, for it leaves the case of the co-adaptations of organic beings to each other and to their physical conditions of life, untouched and unexplained.

This passage disappeared from the third and subsequent editions, suggesting that Chambers, through his complicated channels, had had a quiet word with Darwin.

Instead, in a historical outline, Darwin took a more emollient tone with *Vestiges*:

> The author apparently believes that organisation progresses by sudden leaps, but that the effects produced by the conditions of life are gradual. He argues with much force on general grounds that species are not immutable productions. But I cannot see how the two supposed 'impulses' account in a scientific sense for the numerous and beautiful co-adaptations which we see throughout nature; I cannot see that we thus gain any insight how, for instance, a woodpecker has become adapted to its peculiar habits of life. The work, from its powerful and brilliant style, though displaying in the earlier editions little accurate knowledge and a great want of scientific caution, immediately had a very wide circulation.

No doubt close study had revealed that there was more to *Vestiges* than had seemed at first.

Vestiges had taught Darwin that he needed to be recognised as an authority and that he had to be prepared for vigorous opposition to any view that appeared to run counter to Scripture. He began a project on barnacles which expanded and expanded till it swallowed up eight years of his life, but it gave him personal satisfaction to know that he could go no further and, in addition, that he had been awarded the Royal Society's Medal for his work.

It took 15 years from the publication of *Vestiges* before *Origin* was ready for publication, yet in 1844 he had had 230 pages written. Two factors held him back. One was positive – pride, or professionalism. Whatever he was to produce was to be as perfect as possible. The other was negative – fear of failure, or fear of the contempt of colleagues. Darwin had been circumspect about his *Beagle* material, and in the following years he had suffered a bloody nose over his work on Glen Roy. Chambers had been harried over *Vestiges*. This could not be allowed to happen again.

Eleven years after the first publication of *Vestiges* Darwin could still be diffident, in a letter to Hooker he wrote:

> I should have less scruple in troubling you if I had any confidence what my work would turn out. Sometimes I think it will be good, at other times I really feel as much ashamed of myself as the author of the *Vestiges* ought to be of himself.

As it was, it was the arrival of a paper from Alfred Wallace in the East Indies that galvanised Darwin into action and publication.

Many writers have seen *Vestiges,* in the context of Darwin, worth a mention because he looked at this crude introduction to Evolution and improved upon it. He used it as a means of drawing the poison from reactionary critics. Chambers was John the Baptist, the Forerunner, to Darwin's Messiah.

I prefer Newton's metaphor of the dwarf seated on the shoulders of a giant or, as Coleridge put it: 'The dwarf sees further than the giant, when he has the giant's shoulder to mount on.' The giant, of course, must be Polyphemus, who had only one eye – which matches the imperfect condition of *Vestiges*. While Darwin was no dwarf he certainly benefited from the very substantial beginning made by Chambers to the evolution of serious thought about evolution.

An even better metaphor might be the military one. In the siege of a town or major fortification there came a stage when it was necessary to mount a 'forlorn hope.' In order to reveal and test the defences, a small élite force of volunteers launched a frontal attack, without a preliminary bombardment. There was never any chance of their capturing the city, they were virtually wiped out, but their purpose was served if the besiegers now knew where the strong and weak points in the defences were. *Vestiges of Creation* can be seen as a kind of forlorn hope, it could never have become the sole primer on evolution, but, by testing the defences of the backward-looking establishment, it helped Darwin to make *The Origin of Species* a better book.

Victorian society in the second half of the 19th century was very fortunate in having available parallel justifications for evolution, the classic scientific text of the heroic Darwin, and the readable *Vestiges* by 'a provincial popular author.'

CHAPTER THREE
Three Men in a Boat

IN 1805 JOHN PLAYFAIR described a short journey by boat, carried out by three men of the Enlightenment. They were John Playfair, James Hutton and Sir James Hall and in 1788 they had sailed from Dunglass round the Berwickshire coast to Siccar Point.

FIG 2: Three Men in a Boat

John Playfair's monument on Calton Hill is one of those which helped give Edinburgh its title of 'Athens of the North'. As Professor of Natural Philosophy Playfair (1748–1819) was:

> cast in nature's happiest mould, acute, clear, comprehensive, and having all the higher qualities of intellect combined and regulated by the most perfect good taste, being not less perfect in his moral than in his intellectual nature. He was a man every way distinguished, respected, and beloved. (James Grant, *Cassell's Old and New Edinburgh, vol 2*, no date)

Sir James Hall was the first to demonstrate experimentally how limestone was metamorphosed into marble, while Hutton (1726–97) was a doctor who had studied agriculture and taken up the practical applications of chemistry, moving into geology in 1768.

They landed at Siccar Point and, in one of the finest passages of descriptive prose in the language, Playfair wrote:

> On landing at this point, we found that we actually trode on the primeval rock.
> Dr Hutton was highly pleased with appearances that set in so clear a light the different foundations of the parts which compose the exterior crust of the earth

and proceeded to interpret the 'palpable evidence' that lay before them.

What was this palpable evidence that changed people's view of the past forever? Using the vocabulary of 50 years ago, in Silurian times shales and other rocks were laid down under water. This must have taken a long time.

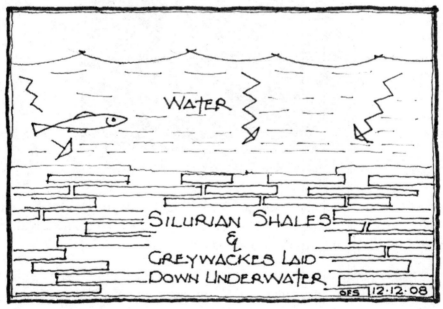

FIG 3: Siccar Point, Phase 1

These rocks were then tilted, uplifted and partially worn away by wind and water. This also would have taken a long time.

FIG 4: Siccar Point, Phase 2

In the Old Red Sandstone period the Silurian rocks were covered by water and more sediments were laid down. These included sandstones and a rock like sandstone which contained fragments from the Silurian rocks. Again, this process must have taken a long time.

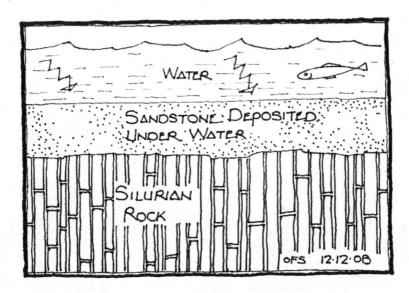

FIG 5: Siccar Point, Phase 3

The line separating the Silurian rocks from the newer sediments above is called an unconformity and represents a period of uplift and erosion, then submergence and deposition. In short, a very long time.

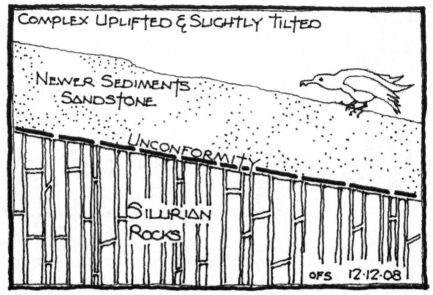

FIG 6: Siccar Point, Phase 4

A street in the Roseburn area of Edinburgh illustrates well what I call an 'urban unconformity', demonstrating the principle in a historical context.

FIG 7: An Urban Unconformity

On the left is a typical tenement block of the 1890s, four storeys in height, stone-built, with minimal front gardens and a forest of chimneys. On the right is a block clearly influenced by the Garden City movement and dating from the 1920s. There are gardens front and rear. The houses are lower, have big bay windows and are of stone-fronted brick. The tenement block was the last to be built in the street, while the villas were the first to be built when house-building restarted in this part of Edinburgh. The sharp division between them – the unconformity – represents a period of 30 years of inactivity in house-building, but of quite frantic change in other parts of the world, not least in the period 1914–18.

The Old Red Sandstone was horizontal and under water when its sediments were accumulating. Now it is slightly tilted and above sea level. This tilting and uplift must also have taken a long time.

Playfair was clearly moved by the processes being revealed to him so clearly:

> We often said to ourselves, What clearer evidence could we have had of the different formation of these rocks, and of the long interval which separated their formation; had we actually seen them emerging from the bosom of the deep?

> We felt ourselves carried back to the time when the schistus was still at the bottom of the sea...

> An epoch still more remote presented itself...

> Revolutions still more remote appeared in the distance of this extraordinary perspective.

> The mind seemed to grow giddy by looking so far into the abyss of time.

Playfair's conclusion was that: 'How much further reason may sometimes go than imagination can venture to follow.'

What strikes the modern observer is how small is the piece of evidence on which Hutton built the theory which shook – and still shakes – the world. Although the whole Siccar Point area has similar features, the classic Hutton's Unconformity takes up little more volume than a decent sized living room. But, as Playfair further wrote:

We were truly fortunate in the course we had pursued in this excursion; a great number of other curious and important facts presented themselves and we returned, having collected, in one day, more ample materials for future speculation than have sometimes resulted from years of diligent and laborious research.

Hutton, of course, was not alone, nor the first, in his speculation about the very fundamental origins of the planet. For him 'the present was the key to the past' – there was no need for supernatural explanations. What was said in the Introduction is worth repeating. Hutton's 'we find no vestige of a beginning, no prospect of an end' was an uncomfortable thought which many, at the time and later, have chosen to misunderstand and which some have still not had the courage to accept.

Famously, or infamously, Bishop James Ussher in 1650 was able to use the Old Testament to say that the world was created on 22 October 4004 BC, a Saturday, about six in the evening. The moment of creation was so precise because the first full day would have had to be a Sunday: 'when the evening and the morning were the first day.' The Jews kept in step, estimating that the same event took place in 3761 BC. For the Muslims the act of creation was of a similar order of magnitude. These dubious authorities were to prove a major obstacle to a rational understanding of natural processes.

In France, Buffon (1707–88), author of the 36-volume *Histoire Naturelle*, was another who was worrying away about the age of the earth and the act of creation. Among much else he studied sedimentation and decided that *'chaque feuillet d'une ardoise correspond à une marée'* (each leaf of a tile – each layer – corresponds with a former sea). He was thus able to calculate: *'qu'une colline de mille toises de hauteur correspond à 14,000 ans de sedimentation.'* A *toise* was about two metres, the French equivalent of a fathom, therefore – assuming the Alps were composed of uniformly uplifted sediments (in itself a pretty big assumption) – the highest mountains of France were about 28,000 years old. The earth was getting older, but there was still a long way to go before Hutton introduced the concept of deep time.

It would be reasonable to expect that Hutton's 'eureka moment' should be commemorated in some suitable way. After all, there are countless memorials to faith in the power of God – great cathedrals and temples, paintings and sculptures, places of pilgrimage, miraculous cures. Hutton's Unconformity, by contrast, rates very low as a tourist attraction. Nobody has the courage or skill today for the approach from the sea. Instead, by a farm track off a minor road, there is an interpretation board showing how to go round two fields, skirting the clifftops to Siccar Point, where one descends a wet slope, as steep as a grassy slope can be without becoming rocky. Great sheets of rough Old Red Sandstone conglomerate are worked over by the North Sea at high tide but, when the tide recedes, a complex pattern of clefts and rock pools is revealed.

It is lonely down here. There may be the occasional fishing boat off-shore but for living companions there are only the shags drying off on the rocks and a few busy waders. Otherwise it is just oneself and the rocks – and one's thoughts. Just like Caspar David Friedrich's lone observer[4]. One can see the same as Hutton did and retrace his line of reasoning. It is easy to step into the shoes of the three earnest philosophers and like them 'to grow giddy by looking so far into the abyss of time.' The believer may look around and say: 'All this was created in six days' – but I cannot see how he could.

However, it does not worry me that there is not a monument at Siccar Point, with the 'Go Giddy with Hutton Experience' and the 'I saw the Unconformity' T-shirt. At Tautavel in Roussillon, the earliest known site of human occupation in Europe, there is a superb interpretative complex from which one can view the excavation site through a high-powered telescope – without trampling all over it. Edinburgh has its Dynamic Earth, another superb interpretation centre using all the modern techniques to recreate the processes Hutton first described and interpreted. In Greyfriars Kirkyard there is a memorial plaque to the 'Founder of Modern Geology' while, between a multi-storey car park and some shabby tenements, the Hutton Memorial Garden marks the site of his house, where *Theory of the Earth* was written. A lump of Triassic sandstone has a cartoon of Hutton and the quotation: 'We find no vestige of a beginning, no prospect of an end.'

FIG 8: Hutton plaque, Hutton Memorial Garden

Around are boulders from Glen Tilt and other localities associated with Hutton. Looming over the site are Salisbury Crags, with Hutton's Section and Hutton's Rock out of sight beyond the Cat's Nick. Stephen Baxter reminds us that 'humans and their petty doings come and go, but the geology endures.'

All over the world are geological exposures – in cliffs and quarries and road cuttings, in the walls of houses and gardens – which can tell a story if we only apply the kind of thinking that Hutton deployed. If, like Playfair, we can realise 'how much further reason may sometimes go than imagination can venture to follow', that is sufficient memorial to a great thinker.

Since that day in 1788 there has been a steady trickle of pilgrims to 'Hutton's Unconformity', not least among them being Charles Lyell who, in 1824, as a keen young geologist, was taken there by Sir James Hall. It was the first volume of Lyell's *Principles of Geology* (1830) which the young Darwin took with him on the *Beagle* and which he said opened his eyes to geology, repeatedly referring to it and the two later volumes, which were sent out to him.

Hutton's *A Theory of the Earth* of 1795 did not immediately command universal acceptance but it certainly caused a ferment of ideas about Creation and the age of the Earth. Many prominent 'philosophers' retained some sort of belief in Biblical creation and catastrophic interventions and vigorously counter-attacked. Hutton died in 1797 and was thus spared much vilification, and having to read Kirwan's *Geological Essays* of 1799. Playfair took up the cause on behalf of Hutton and his ideas.

By the time that Darwin came to Edinburgh University, although Playfair had died in 1819, there would still have been a scientific community who had known Playfair and his campaigns on behalf of Hutton's ideas, and who tacitly accepted the evidence and arguments for a very distant creation and a long, slow geological history. There was still, however, a kernel of prominent diehards. Such were Cuvier in France, Werner in Germany and Professor Jameson in Edinburgh, teaching the geology course, which was 'the largest course of its type in the world.'

Charles Darwin (1808–82) followed his elder brother Erasmus to Edinburgh University in 1825, at the age of 16, and spent two academic sessions here as a medical student.

Darwin found the lectures 'intolerably dull.' 'Dr Duncan's lectures on Materia Medica at 8 o'clock on a winter's morning are something fearful to remember.' 'Dr [Monro] made his lectures on human anatomy as dull as he was himself.' On two occasions Darwin was present at 'very bad operations' and 'rushed away before they were completed. ... Nor did I ever attend again.' He considered that 'there are no advantages and many disadvantages in lectures compared with reading.'

In the second year Robert Jameson, Professor of Natural History, which then included zoology and geology, was 'incredibly dull.'

> The sole effect they produced on me was the determination never as long as I lived to read a book on Geology, or in any way to study the science.

In the *Autobiography* he let himself go on the subject of Jameson:

> Equally striking is the fact that I though now only 67 years old heard Prof. Jameson in a field lecture at Salisbury Craigs discoursing on a trap-dyke, with amygdaloidal margins and the strata indurated on each side, with volcanic rocks all around us, and say that it was a fissure filled with sediment from above, adding with a sneer that there were men who maintained that it

had been injected from beneath in a molten condition. When I think of this lecture I do not wonder that I determined never to attend to Geology.

That Darwin's dislike of Jameson was lifelong and not merely an attitude recollected from notes in old age is shown by a letter (Number 899 in the Darwin Correspondence Project) he wrote to Lyell in 1845, when Darwin was 36:

> ...all the arguments in the world on your side are not equal to one course of Jameson's lectures on the other side, which I formerly for my sins experienced.

On the positive side, Darwin was elected first to the Plinian Natural History Society, then to its Council (of five). In the *Autobiography* he says: 'The Plinian Society was encouraged and I believe founded by Professor Jameson.' The 'incredibly dull' Professor Jameson. The young Charles attended all but one of the 19 meetings held during his time at Edinburgh and took part in discussion on four of the evenings. Papers read included the alleged ovi-position of the cuckoo in the nests of other birds, extra-uterine gestation, the results of the analysis of the Cheltenham waters, oceanic and atmospheric currents, the anatomy of expression, the various purposes to which the formation of a vacuum is applied in the animal kingdom, instinct, and the natural history of the cuckoo. An eclectic programme.

He communicated to the Society two discoveries he had made. He was also a member of the Royal Medical Society and attended pretty regularly. 'Much rubbish was talked there.' And:

> Dr Grant took me occasionally to the meetings of the Wernerian Society. I heard Audubon deliver there some interesting discourses on the habits of North American birds.

(Wernerians were 'Neptunists', believing that all rocks were laid down under water. Jameson was clearly a Wernerian and on Salisbury Crags was taking a sly dig at the late Dr Hutton, Plutonist and author of *The Theory of the Earth*).

The Plinian Society was a strong influence on the young Darwin and, as we shall see, one of the meetings occupied his mind for over 40 years before he set it down in a very strange book.

Dr Robert Grant (who became the first Professor of Zoology in University College, London) was Secretary of the Plinian Society and a considerable influence on Darwin. Many years later, Darwin was to write, with a degree of ambiguity:

> ...Dr Grant, my senior by several years, but how I became acquainted with him I cannot remember. He published some first-rate zoological papers, but after coming to London as Professor in University College he did nothing more in science, a fact which has always been inexplicable to me.

With zoology (rather than geology) as a focus they investigated together the shores of the Forth at Leith, Portobello, Joppa and (it is said) Dalmeny/Queensferry. Although two of these localities are now classic excursions of the Edinburgh Geological Society the nearest we find of thinking beyond straightforward description and identification is a reported outburst by Grant on Lamarck and his views on evolution. Darwin listened in 'silent astonishment' but does not seem to have let it affect him at the time.

Jean-Baptiste Pierre Antoine de Monet, chevalier de Lamarck (1744–1829) was a force to be reckoned with in his time. (Grant spent five years in Paris and may well have come under Lamarck's influence when there.) He coined the term 'biology' for the new science of natural history and believed that species could 'transmute,' could evolve from one to another (unlike Cuvier, who maintained that species remained unchanged from the time of the creation). He also believed that acquired characteristics could be passed on the next generation.

To take an obvious example, when we think of the giraffe we observe that it lives off spiny acacia leaves which it must stretch up to in order to graze. (It also has an 18-inch tongue). In its neck the giraffe has the same seven bones as we have, or the mouse has, but longer, and common sense tells us that giraffes have been grazing high and stretching out and that each generation has carried on the process further. But common sense is not always correct. Common sense and observation tell us that the sun rises in the east and moves round the earth till it sets in the west – every day – yet we know that it is we who are spinning around the sun. For the giraffe we have the problem that the adult male is considerably bigger than the female – Are there different trees for each gender? Why have the females not died out?

Lamarckism was an attractive form of evolution – but new behavioural patterns do not produce inheritable bodily changes; a blacksmith's children do not inherit the iron-band arms their father developed. (Although they may develop a similar physique by training and through example).

There is a puzzle, however, about this incident with Grant and why, 50 years after the event, Darwin chose to record it. What was he trying to prove? Did he think that, even at this late date, some critic might seek to question his own version of evolution? Was there something discreditable about Grant that Darwin sought to dissociate himself from? And if so, why mention the incident at all?

There is no doubt that Darwin was a good student. He attended the classes, however dull. He took part in cognate activities beyond the core curriculum. He kept a good note-book ('perhaps slight, as judged by modern standards'). But the experience was not enjoyable for him and he did not realise that part of a medicine course was learning not to be sickened by the horrors of early 19th century surgery. He was fortunate to have a father understanding and wealthy enough to allow him to drop medicine at Edinburgh in favour of the more congenial BA course at Christ's College, Cambridge.

Some writers make much of his squeamishness at operations, but the same fastidious Darwin, when he was in Edinburgh, took lessons in taxidermy from: 'a blackamoor I believe an old servant of Dr Duncan' – a negro ex-slave. 'John' had arrived in Glasgow from Guyana in 1817 and settled in the University Museum, where he gave lessons to genteel young shooters who wanted to stuff their trophies. For one guinea, Darwin had the company of a black man for an hour a day for two months, an enlightening experience for the time and one he used well: 'I used often to sit with him, for he was a very pleasant and intelligent man,' as he recorded in his *Autobiography*. A good sporting shot in his student days, when Darwin was on the *Beagle* voyage he hunted for food for the wardroom as well as shooting specimens, stuffing them and sending them back to England.

We can see in this relationship an openness unsurprising in one of an extended family devoted to the anti-slavery cause. If nothing else, Darwin was to learn in Edinburgh that it was possible for a black man to make a living in white society through the application of his intelligence and that it was also possible for white and black to co-exist in society, and could set this beside the horrifying experiences he was later to have in Brazil.

For Darwin's student days there are three main sources. His notebook, begun in March 1827, has survived. His *Autobiography,* started in 1876 – when he was 67 – and added to in 1878 and 1881, devotes six pages to his Edinburgh days. J.H. Ashworth, Professor of Zoology at Edinburgh, in 1935 gave a substantial paper of 19 pages on *Charles Darwin as a Student in Edinburgh, 1825–1827.* Here emerges the question of reliability of evidence. The notebook is an objective record of observations and excursions. There may be errors of identification but the result must be near the truth as Darwin saw it at the time.

Later we shall come across Patrick Geddes. Most of what we know of his early days comes from two sources. In 1923 Geddes gave a series of lectures in the United States, which were published in 1925, when he was 71. He was trying to prove that the *Education of Two Boys* he had undergone was a model to be copied. I do not suggest that Geddes lied, but from our own experiences, we know how selective memory can be, and I have no doubt that Geddes's memory was conveniently selective. When Geddes was 74 (in 1928) his old school magazine published *Memories and Reflections,* written at Montpellier, which seemed to suggest that his school days were not so very different from the norm of the time.

As with Geddes we should also be conscious that Darwin was 67 when his *Autobiography* was published and therefore exercise suitable caution with its interpretation. Ashworth picked up at least one error of fact:

> His communication to the Plinian Society was on March 27, 1827, not 'at the beginning of the year 1826' as stated in the *Autobiography.*

This may be pettifogging, nitpicking and too trivial to be concerned about. Or it may be the tip of an iceberg of prejudice.

Gavin de Beer, editor of the *Autobiography,* had this to say on the subject of recollection:

> With Darwin's *Autobiography,* as we shall see, there is a comparable discrepancy between his memory and the day-to-day records of the development of his ideas and thoughts.

A common feature of good autobiographies is that they do not lend themselves readily to collation with journals and diaries kept by the writers at earlier times of their lives.

The writer can see things out of focus with an aberration magnified by hindsight which might lead him astray.

Huxley was characteristically direct: 'Autobiographies are essentially works of fiction, whatever biographies may be.'

There is a clear disparity between Darwin's recollections of his Edinburgh studies and the experiences of contemporaries almost as able as he was. Darwin's opinion of much of his course work was 'dull, dull, dull.' Other gifted students of the same period did not necessarily agree. Robert (later Sir Robert, successive occupant of two medical chairs at Edinburgh) Christison found that Monro:

gave a very clear, precise, complete course of lectures on anatomy …and certainly I learned anatomy well under him.

The 'incredibly dull' Jameson had been Professor of Natural History for 22 years and covered mineralogy, zoology and geology. He edited the *Edinburgh Philosophical Journal* and the *New Philosophical Journal* and developed an extensive and important Natural History Museum in the University. Notable for:

the excellent state of preservation of its specimens and their scientific arrangement and for its large collection of birds,

the entire museum collection, 'second only to that of the British Museum', was handed over to the new Government Museum of Science and Art, later the Royal Scottish Museum and now the Royal Museum of Scotland, a year after his death. (Ashworth, *Darwin in Edinburgh, 1825–27. 1935*). He attacked Hutton in print and before his students in the field – Salisbury Crags. On Hutton's death his specimen collection passed to the University Museum, where it was not displayed and gradually disappeared.

In the course that Darwin took in his second year there were about 100 lectures, five days a week, 'conversations' with the Professor in the Museum and excursions. Edward Forbes took Professor Jameson's course in 1832 and succeeded him as Professor in 1854. He found 'Jameson's collection wonderful, even palaeontologically' and the illustrative material 'very great.' He spoke of his Professor's 'enthusiastic zeal, his wonderful acquaintance with scientific literature.' More –

> The value of professorial worth should chiefly be estimated by the number and excellence of disciples. A large share of the best naturalists of the day received their first instruction in the science from Professor Jameson...And where else in the British Empire, except here, has there been for the last half century a school of Natural History?

Christison attended the course of 1816, when:

> Lectures were numerously attended in spite of a dry manner, and although attendance on Natural History was not enforced for any University honour or for any profession, the popularity of his subject, his earnestness as a lecturer, his enthusiasm as an investigator, and the great museum he had collected for illustrating his teaching, were together the causes of his success.

Later, in the context of Darwin's suitability for the *Beagle* project, Desmond and Moore in *Darwin* rather patronisingly concede that 'Jameson's Edinburgh course, as luck would have it, had catered for colonial travellers.' Luck had nothing to do with it. Jameson's course was a vocational one aimed at equipping young men with the wherewithal to make their way in the world furth of Scotland. (In their *Darwin's Sacred Cause* of 2009 they make amends by analysing Jameson's course: 'a course packed with the next generation of travellers: surveyors, civil engineers and army surgeons.')

Why was Cambridge more congenial? Darwin was, of course, more mature: with the experience behind him of working at something he did not enjoy. He must have responded better to the relaxed English way, as opposed to the stern drive of the lean and hungry Scots. At Edinburgh he had lodged in the town; college life at Cambridge suited 'a young man with easy manners and a cheerful disposition who could ride and shoot.'

We hear little of his course work but can see developing a Cambridge University network which stood him well in later years.

What he did not have in Cambridge was a cultural life of any quality. In far-off Edinburgh the first performance of *Der Freischütz* by Carl Maria von Weber[5] had taken place on 29 December 1824. Miss Stephens, a leading soprano of the time, had been 'quite delightful.' The young Charles Darwin, writing to his father on 23 October 1825, said: 'On Monday we are going to Der Fr. (I do not know how to spell the rest of the word).' One wonders how the tone-deaf Darwin might have reacted to 'Agathe's outburst of joy when she sees her lover approaching.' It has been suggested that Emma Darwin's playing the piano of an evening had a greater effect than mere relaxation.

The mature Darwin was a rational observer and recorder. Could it be that, underneath, there was a touch of the Romantic? We do not know how he reacted to the Wolf's Glen and the Satanic casting of magical bullets, but in *The Voyage of the* Beagle there are at least two moments capable of a Romantic interpretation.

How, then, if Stephen Baxter is correct, did Darwin manage to avoid absorbing the concept of 'deep time' during his two years at Edinburgh? I think there are two explanations, one very simple and another more mysterious.

When I was young there were many young lads – seldom girls – who collected the numbers and names of railway engines, who could go on for hours about A4 Pacifics, Stanier Black Fives and the Scott class and could even spell 'Walschaert's Valve Gear', without conceptualising their knowledge by asking questions like: Why? or Why there? Similarly, Darwin's enthusiasm at 16 was for observing and collecting in the field – 'bug-hunting' – rather than for concern about the big picture. It was there, sketch it or kill it and write it up. Why speculate about how it got there?

For much of the 20th century Jean Piaget's ideas about how children learn held sway. He saw an array of concepts, each to be mastered in turn as children developed. The good teacher understood that there was a 'readiness for learning' to be recognised and utilised in a progressive way.

With no commitment to medicine as a career, Darwin may quite simply have been unready for the full understanding of the studies offered to him. Yet his time at Edinburgh was not wasted, because he acquired there – despite his lack of enthusiasm – the basic skills of scientific investigation without losing his enthusiasm for natural history.

So much for the simple explanation. The other must wait for the next episode.

CHAPTER FOUR

Silent, upon a peak in Darien

FOR ME, 11 JANUARY 2002 was very special. On that day I was in La Campana National Park, Chile, covering some of the territory that Darwin covered on 16 and 17 August 1834; experiencing for myself four separate aspects of the observational powers which were recorded in pages 208 to 211 of *Journal of Researches into the Geology and Natural History of the Various Countries visited by* HMS Beagle.

HMS *Beagle,* under the command of Robert Fitzroy (promoted from Commander to Captain during the voyage) circumnavigated the globe, setting out from Plymouth on 27 December 1831 and dropping anchor on her return to Falmouth on 2 October 1836. The purpose of the voyage was to complete the survey of the coast of southern South America. Darwin joined the ship as gentleman companion and naturalist, was not a member of the crew or under naval orders and was financed by his father. *Beagle* spent spells of varying length surveying and in port and at these times Darwin made expeditions on land: of the almost five years of the voyage only about eighteen months (533 days) were spent at sea by Darwin.

My main source has been the Penguin Classics edition of *Voyage of the* Beagle, which has two main inbuilt disadvantages. In order to bring Darwin's work into a Penguin format it was necessary to shorten the text by about one-third. On the voyage Darwin made 1,383 pages of notes on geology, as compared to 368 pages on zoology. Passages that the editors thought would be 'unlikely to be missed' were excised. To give one example, the summary at the start of Chapter XII includes:

> Wolf-like fox – *Fire made of bones – Art in making fire – Manner of hunting wild cattle – Geology, fossil shells –* Valleys filled with great fragments, scenes of violence.

In the text the headings italicised are replaced by three asterisks. Most of the 'geology bit' has disappeared. This is particularly irritating since

Chapter XII was set in the Falkland Islands, where current research into the fossils is proving very interesting.

The second problem is that, if poetry is emotion recollected in tranquillity, Darwin's South American geology is observation recollected in a distant study. Darwin kept a detailed diary during the voyage but it was seven months after his return to England before it was published. *Voyage of the* Beagle appeared in 1839, three years after her return. Thus there was ample scope for reflection and what we read was most unlikely to have been what Darwin felt, or thought, on the spot. We can be sure that he was conscious that whatever appeared in print would be subject to close scrutiny.

Nevertheless, we can still make a qualitative assessment of Darwin's attitude towards 'deep time' from the *Voyage*, an assessment of what he wanted us to believe rather than what he actually did believe. Thus, in Chapter I, at Bahia in Brazil, he wonders:

> Can we believe that any power acting for a time short of infinity could have denuded the granite over so many thousand square leagues?

There is often a 'wood and trees' problem. In Patagonia, for example, Darwin describes variations in beach levels, and variations in 12 species of shellfish in some kind of order – but no more. He lists fossil remains of 13 quadrupeds which:

> co-existed during an epoch which, geologically speaking, is so recent, that it may be considered as only just gone by.

Near Bahia Blanca there is some observation of quartz, slate and a conglomerate, with a little mild speculation as to how the last was deposited, but little that one can seize upon. Near Montevideo he describes a section indicating successive deposition of clay and limestone, with marine remains shading off into an estuary deposit – but no timetable.

Again in Patagonia, Darwin considers the formation of raised beaches, using such phrases as 'a long period of repose,' 'periods of rest,' 'insensibly rising,' 'a steady but very gradual elevation' – so vague as to be almost meaningless. Within sight of the high peaks of the Cordillera he describes the very varied size and composition of erratic blocks without any acceptable explanation of their derivation.

In the Falklands Darwin came across 'streams of stones' – periglacial blockfields as we would now call them – which he described in meticulous detail, speculating as to their formation. Was

> a great arched fragment fairly pitched up in the air and thus turned? Or was this fragment the last vestige of an earlier surface whose debris have been shaken by innumerable earthquakes into one continuous sheet?

His conclusion, that

> never did any scene...so forcibly convey to my mind the idea of a convulsion of which in historical records we might in vain seek for any counterpart,

seems to be groping around the ideas that 'the present is the key to the past' and of an enormously long time-scale.

By February 1834 the *Beagle* and Darwin had rounded the Horn and were at Valdivia, in Chile. On the 20th Darwin was on shore and was lying down in a wood to rest himself when:

> A most severe earthquake...came on suddenly, and lasted two minutes, but the time appeared much longer. The rocking of the ground was most sensible.

He described the undulations of the ground and the strange feeling of insecurity, but saw little damage. However, Captain Fitzroy and his officers were in the town and witnessed a great deal of destruction, with many walls running from NW to SE 'thrown down...nearly coincident to the line of undulation,' pointing to 'the SW as the chief focus of disturbance' – what we would now call the epicentre.

On 4 March they entered the harbour of Concepcion:

> Not a house in Concepcion was standing...70 villages were destroyed...a great wave had almost washed away the ruins of Talcuhano.

There had been a tsunami as well as the earthquake proper and Darwin spends several pages describing and analysing the damage.

He did not attempt a detailed description of the appearance of

Concepcion, instead, with some honesty, confesses to forgetting almost instantly compassion for the inhabitants in favour of:

> ...the interest excited in finding that state of things produced in a moment of time, which one is accustomed to attribute to a succession of ages. In my opinion, we have scarcely beheld since leaving England, any other sight so deeply interesting.

Darwin's first-hand experience of the earthquake, the tsunami and 'the permanent elevation of the land' had a great influence on Darwin's thinking. There he was, beginning to come to terms with a world subject to long, slow processes operating over a long time scale, when he was presented with the proof that there were also catastrophic events resulting in 'the permanent elevation of the land.' As we shall see, it was to take a long time for Darwin to reconcile properly in his own mind these seemingly contradictory processes and to appreciate that what appears to be, in human terms, a swift and violent catastrophe in geological terms is a tiny incident in a long, slow sequence of processes.

16 and 17 August 1834 are important in highlighting four aspects of Darwin's work and legacy. On these days Darwin ascended the Campana (or Bell mountain, 6,400 feet) in what is now La Campana National Park.

FIG 9: La Campana National Forest, Palm Forest

He saw and gave a page to the Chilean Palm (*Jubaea chilensis*) which here forms the most southerly palm forest in the world (at 32' 57" south, 71' 05" west). 'Excessively numerous' in Darwin's time, its population has declined from five million to only 124,000 today. It is a sobering thought to look around the National Park and see two-thirds of the world's population of this impressive tree, and to realise that some of the finest old specimens must have been seen, if not noticed, by Darwin on that special day.

Unusually, for whatever reason, Darwin says more about this one tree than any other single plant on his travels. He does not 'do' conservation in his *Journal* and could not have been expected to forecast the near extinction of this sugar palm, but his extended description of the methods used in the extraction of the sugar makes it clear to us that this was not a sustainable operation.

We are familiar with Darwin the bug-hunter, the barnacle man; on La Campana he becomes the romantic traveller, revelling in the sunset, the bird song and the pleasures of the open air life. By day there is the splendid beauty of the Andes and the superb clarity of the air – the masts of the

FIG 10: Chilean Sugar Palm (*Jubaea chilensis*)

ships in the harbour at Valparaiso, 26 miles away, can be picked out – inspiring thoughts of the Sublime.

The poet Keats had no Greek and had to wait for an English translation of *The Odyssey* before he could appreciate its greatness. In *On First Looking into Chapman's Homer* he describes the excitement of a completely new discovery:

> Then felt I like some watcher of the skies
> When a new planet swims into his ken;
> Or like stout Cortes when with eagle eyes
> He star'd at the Pacific – and all his men
> Look'd at each other with a wild surmise –
> Silent, upon a peak in Darien.

Never mind the poetic licence – it was Balboa, not 'stout' Cortes, who was the first European to see the Pacific – Darwin must have had the same feeling as he saw from on high the vastness of the Pacific, the hugeness of the Andes and the implied depth of our very existence. 'Wild surmise' was exactly right, one feels.

Darwin the observer and recorder was not idle, however. He noted that the summit of the mountain was made of huge angular fragments of basalt which 'presented every degree of freshness' and hypothesised about this and the later contrast with Mount Wellington near Hobart.

Here, also, Darwin finally began to make clear a commitment to the concept of 'deep time':

> Who can avoid admiring the wonderful force which has upheaved these mountains, and even more so the countless ages which it must have required, to have broken through, removed and levelled whole masses of them?

although a convoluted double negative – a reflection of uncertainty? – rather dilutes a later statement that all-powerful time can grind down mountains – even the gigantic Cordillera – into gravel and mud.

Seven months later, in the same district, he wrote:

> These mountains have existed as a great barrier, since a period so remote that whole races of animals must subsequently have perished from the face of the earth.

(Yet we, with the smugness of hindsight, know that the Andes are, in world terms, really rather young mountains, having developed only over the last 50 million years!)

30 April 1835 was the day on which Darwin had his own 'eureka moment', reminiscent of Playfair's account of Hutton's revelation at Siccar Point:

> It required little geological practice to interpret the marvellous story, which this scene at once unfolded, though I confess I was at first so much astonished that I could scarcely believe the plainest evidence of it.

Like Hutton, he enumerated each step in the evolution of the landscape of his time, concluding:

Vast and scarcely comprehensible as such changes must ever appear, yet they have all occurred within a period recent when compared with the history of the Cordillera; and that Cordillera itself is modern as compared with some other of the fossiliferous strata of South America.

Back in Cambridge, John Henslow was Regius Professor of Botany. Thirteen years older than Darwin, he was, to a certain degree, Darwin's mentor, patron and scientific godfather. It was to Henslow that much of Darwin's collected material was despatched and Darwin constantly sought Henslow's approval. During the voyage he and Darwin corresponded and on 12 August 1835, in a long letter, Darwin slipped in some revealing phrases.

Since his last letter he had 'seen something more of the Cordilleras.' Some of his 'Geological views' had been 'subsequently to the last letter altered.' He believed that 'the upper mass of strata' were 'not so very modern' as he had supposed. Without mentioning a time-scale he implies extremely lengthy processes: 'enormous streams of lava' alternating with 'sedimentary beds to a vast thickness,' 'strata several thousand feet thick of coarse Conglomerate,' 'alternations of compact crystalline rocks...and sedimentary beds, now upheaved, fractured and indurated.' Henslow read some of Darwin's letters to the Philosophical Society of Cambridge and had them printed for private distribution. Small wonder that Darwin was circumspect in what he wrote. That Darwin was probably right to be tactful emerged much later when, in the aftermath of *Origin of Species,* Henslow fell out with Darwin.

If Stephen Baxter is correct it would seem that Darwin sailed on the *Beagle* with an outmoded set of ideas. Darwin himself attributed his development as a geologist to Lyell and his *Principles of Geology.* His *Journal* suggests a long period of gestation until he was prepared to declare publicly his acceptance of 'deep time.' We know how cautious, even diffident, Darwin could be, seeking the approval of Henslow and others. He sat on the *Beagle*-inspired ideas on the *Origin of Species* for many years before an imminent publication by Wallace forced him into action.

One always feels sorry for poor Wallace. He had none of the advantages Darwin had fallen heir to. Always running like mad to stay in the same place, he felt he had to defer to Darwin and other patrons. A self-taught socialist and professional plant collector, 'through the tropics he carried the evolutionary *Vestiges of Creation* in his mental kit' say Desmond and Moore in *Darwin's Sacred Cause*. *Vestiges* had predicted where 'the cradle of the human family' was located, so Wallace buried himself in the Dutch East Indies. 'Ten thousand miles from home, Wallace rushed in where Darwin feared to write', only to be outmanoeuvred by the Cambridge establishment in the run-up to *Origin of Species*. Yet he threw himself consistently into valuable enterprises. Having worked and lived with 'his subjects' in the East Indies he had much valuable observation for Darwin to use in *Expression of the Emotions* – practical information which Darwin, sitting at Down, found difficult to reconcile with his memories of Tierra del Fuego, his prejudices and second-hand anecdotes.

In *Darwin* Desmond and Moore narrate an incident which reflects little credit on Darwin. In the early 1870s Darwin approached Wallace: 'struggling as a self-financed writer and in need of work', with a view to using him to revise the *Descent of Man*. Wallace had helped Lyell to edit his *Principles of Geology* for five shillings (25 pence) an hour – low pay for 'the class of work' – and quoted seven shillings (35 pence). Emma Darwin put a stop to the deal and persuaded Darwin to give the job to George, their 25-year-old son, who would do it for nothing, but had no competence in the field.

An even more sheepish Darwin told Wallace that if 'my son could not do the work, I will write again and *gratefully* accept your proposal.'

In my young days every good atlas showed 'Wallace's Line' snaking between Bali and Lombok and through the East Indies between Borneo and the Celebes. It separated the flora and fauna of Asia from that of Australasia – in effect the former Pangea and Gondwanaland. In our present world of satellite imagery and remote sensing there is no room for poor old Wallace's Line, which has been rubbed out. Yet Wallace's work was fundamental as one of the earliest providers of evidence for the theory of Continental Drift.

Darwin avoided time-wasting and often contentious committees and the like (although he reluctantly took up the Secretaryship of the Geological Society). Later in life, when things got too hot he took to his bed, or took himself off to Dr Gully's Water Cure Hotel at Great Malvern and left the public fight to Hooker and Huxley.

Dr Gully[6] was another Edinburgh student who went on to edit a radical London newspaper, translated Tiedemann's *Comparative Physiology* and in later years became Darwin's physician.

In a recent broadcast in Melvyn Bragg's Radio 4 series 'In Our Time,' much was made of the steamy nature of Cambridge life in Darwin's time. A squalid 'Town' served a hormonally active 'Gown' of young males ruled by senior members of the Established Church of England, sunk in intellectual lethargy. The Reverend Adam Sedgwick, as Senior Proctor, was responsible for applying the double standard of sending the naughty girls to the House of Correction while the young bloods who paid for their services were given a wigging or rusticated for a term or so. A quarter of Darwin's fellow medical students at Edinburgh were English, unable or unwilling to attend Oxford or Cambridge for reasons of religion but welcome in a city where, with

FIG 11: Dr James Manby Gully practised the Malvern Water Cure here 1842–72

all its faults, the clergy – in the 1820s – had mainly contrived to balance scientific thinking with religious principle.

At Cambridge Darwin had been on a course which would have meant conformity with and eventual subscription to the 39 Articles of 1571. Whatever Darwin thought about deep time, he had to conform on the surface to the society around him. Many years later, the reaction of Sedgwick to *Origin of Species* was: 'I have read your book with more pain than pleasure.' Reverend Professor Henslow (Mineralogy, 1822, Botany 1825) was made Rector of Hitcham in 1839. An excellent clergyman, complaints were made within the university of neglect of his duties there. With mentors like these it is understandable that Darwin felt it necessary to keep his cards close to his chest.

It could be that Darwin was quite content to play the part of Expedition Naturalist, to record and collect, to send plant and animal material home, and, quite simply, keep out of areas where nothing but controversy would result.

I should like to conclude this section by examining a series of episodes, on either side of the *Beagle* voyage and spread over 11 years, which others have described but do not seem to have considered worth commenting on, but which I find very difficult to understand.

Darwin was a favourite student of Adam Sedgwick, Professor of Geology and President of the Geological Society of London. In 1831 Sedgwick planned a visit to North Wales to clear up some problems of the region. Darwin 'worked like a tiger at geology' and was taken along as assistant and pupil. The pair spent a week on fieldwork, working separately during the day and pooling their information in the evenings, trying to clarify what had happened in the area before the Old Red Sandstone was laid down.

Darwin knew his Sedgwick. The discovery of a tropical Volute shell in a gravel pit near Shrewsbury elicited from Sedgwick the remark that, had it been really embedded there, it would be the greatest misfortune to geology, as it would overthrow all that we know about the superficial deposits of the midland counties. Darwin:

> was then utterly astonished at Sedgwick not being delighted at so wonderful a fact as a tropical shell being found near the surface in the middle of England.

On this tour, as he called it, he had a striking instance of how easy it was to overlook phenomena, however conspicuous, before they have been observed by anyone.

> We spent many hours in Cwm Idwall, examining all the rocks with extreme care, as Sedgwick was anxious to find fossils in them; but neither of us saw a trace of the wonderful glacial phenomena all around us; we did not notice the plainly scored rocks, the perched boulders, the lateral and terminal moraines. Yet these phenomena are so conspicuous that...a house burnt down by fire did not tell its story more plainly than did this valley. If it had still been filled by a glacier; the phenomena would have been less distinct than they now are.

Then, in South America, he came across the full expression of mountain glaciation – frost-shattered arêtes, corries, roches moutonnées, U-shaped and hanging valleys, ribbon lakes, moraines, erratics, outwash and the rest.

In 1838 his 'eight good days in Glen Roy' tried to solve the riddle of the Parallel Roads, based on his South American experience, only for him to end up in an intellectual cul-de-sac.

In 1842 he returned to North Wales. In his own words:

> Eleven years ago, I spent a whole day in the valley, where yesterday everything but the ice of the glacier was palpably clear to me, and then I saw nothing but plain water and bare rock.

Darwin attributed his new clarity of vision to his reading – particularly Lyell – but surely his own practical experience should have been crucial to his new understanding. And what was his mentor, the Professor of Geology at the University of Cambridge and President of the Geological Society of London, doing in 1831 when the pair of them were sorting out the day's findings?

Did he know that J. Esmark in Norway had published a paper in Norway in 1824 demonstrating that Norway had been covered by an ice sheet? And that this had been republished in the *Edinburgh New Philosophical Journal* in 1827? And that the despised Jameson – editor of that journal – was already, in 1827:

> ...suggesting to his students the possibility that the transported blocks of rock that occur widely in Scotland had been carried by glaciers
>
> (*The Evolution of Scotland's Scenery*, Sissons, 1967)

and that he 'expressed the view in his lectures that glaciers had once existed in Scotland' (*Land of Mountain and Flood: The Geology and Landforms of Scotland*, McKirdy, Gordon and Crofts, 2007)?

And if Sedgwick did not know these things, how could he claim to be 'a man of science', the term he used when he was castigating Chambers in 1844? Were he and Darwin so concerned about fossils and the detailed composition of the rocks that they could not stand up and look around at the big landscape around them?

Patrick Geddes was no great shakes as a writer, his prose style being reminiscent of Thomas Carlyle on an off-day. Yet he had the gift of being able to coin new words which have entered the language, like 'conurbation,' and he could come up with the telling or quotable phrase. Geddes, who contributed an article on 'Variation and Selection' to *Encyclopaedia Britannica*, probably had Darwin in mind when he stated that, pre-*Origin of Species*, there was:

> a tendency to concentrate upon more concrete and smaller problems alone, since of these the solution was comparatively sure.

In addition, Darwin knew on which side his bread was buttered and kept his cards close to his chest on matters which might cause difficulty.

CHAPTER FIVE

Charles Lyell –
the Long Way Round

LIKE DARWIN, CHARLES LYELL was born into a privileged position in society. Like Darwin also, Lyell was a gifted amateur who was destined for another career but turned to science where he made a major impact. Their career trajectories differed. Unlike Darwin, Lyell made his most important contribution early, at the age of 33, but nothing that he did subsequently, however distinguished, matched the *Principles of Geology*. Darwin was 50 when *Origin of Species* was published and still had much illuminating work to come. When one thinks of Hutton it is with respect tinged with affection. With Darwin it is respect tinged with occasional irritation, but Lyell one thinks of with respect mixed with frustration.

Charles Lyell (1797–1875), Scottish geologist, was born at Kinnordy House, near Kirriemuir, in the year that Hutton died. He was the son of a keen botanist and Dante scholar with a large, well-stocked library, where the young Charles browsed and developed an interest in natural history. In the late 19th century a small Scottish town, like Kirriemuir, would typically have been served by 'the three kirks' – 'the Auld Kirk' (Church of Scotland), the Free Kirk and the UP Kirk (United Presbyterian, an amalgamation of smaller churches which had seceded or been expelled from the Church of Scotland) – all Presbyterian. Increasingly, the process of Anglicisation saw the gentry and socially aspiring moving into the Anglican church, the Episcopal Church in Scotland, which had bishops, vestments and music like its opposite number in England. When the minister of St Cuthbert's in Edinburgh denounced the first issue of *Chambers Journal* from the pulpit it was into the Scottish Episcopalians that Anne and Robert Chambers moved. While the Presbyterian clergy had found it possible to reconcile scientific thinking with the Biblical narrative a young Scots Anglican would have found it easy to blend in with a church which had yet to solve this problem.

However, Lyell was no typical Scottish laird's son, rather he was an

Anglo-Scot. His father, also Charles, had inherited the large Angus estate but continued to have a family home in Hampshire. Thus young Charles grew up with a foot in both camps; a stance that was to be typical in later life. James Secord sums up his background in a few phrases. Lyell's father was an 'opponent of reform', of the 'moderate Tory gentry'. His sisters 'were hated as Tory gentry'. At the height of the Reform Bill agitation there was a by-election in Forfarshire. The rest of the family canvassed for the Tories and young Lyell abstained. When he took up a Chair of Geology in 1831 'it was at King's College, founded by Anglican Tories to counter the utilitarian University of London.' Trying to make a living by writing about geology, says Secord in *Victorian Sensation*:

> Lyell reviewed for the Tory *Quarterly* not the Whig *Edinburgh*, where reforming views on education and science had been trumpeted for decades.

His great book, *Principles of Geology,* was brought out by '[John] Murray, a Tory publisher.'

Lyell read classics at Oxford, but attended geology lectures on an extra-curricular basis. The Rev William Buckland inspired him with a romantic picture of strange creatures adapting to extreme physical conditions, all consequent upon divine creation as described in Genesis and the universal Deluge. He moved to London, intending to qualify to become a barrister, but 'push-pull' factors determined that he should try a new career as a science writer. The push was that his eyesight was already deteriorating (he went completely blind later in life). The pull was that he could exercise his talent for writing, which had emerged at Oxford. James Secord, this time in his Introduction to the Penguin Classics edition of Lyell's *Principles of Geology* states that writing about science was an activity worthy of a gentleman:

> Since a gentleman's right to independent judgement was acknowledged, he remained welcome both at home and in fashionable Tory circles in the metropolis.

In 1824 he was taken to Siccar Point and Hutton's Unconformity by Sir James Hall, one of the 'Three Men in a Boat' of 1788. We do not know how Lyell reacted to his field visit, but he immersed himself in the writings of John Playfair (the third 'man in the boat'), particularly *Illustrations on the Huttonian Theory of the Earth*. He does not seem to have read Hutton for himself, relying on Playfair's intercession for his information.

The young Darwin was in Edinburgh at this time but did not make it to Siccar Point. Had he done so, things might have been different. He might have become aware of 'deep time' directly from the concrete evidence. Instead, there was a kind of Apostolic Succession as the message was passed from Hutton to Hall and Playfair, from Hall and Playfair to Lyell, and from Lyell to Darwin by means of *Principles of Geology: being an Attempt to explain the Former Changes of the Earth's Surface, by Reference to Causes now in Operation*. Thus the understanding of deep time came to Darwin the long way round.

In the 19th century a substantial book like the *Principles* was not published as one blockbuster but in manageable parts. Darwin took Volume I with him on the *Beagle* and repeatedly referred to it, saying that it had opened his eyes to geology – and this from a man who had 'determined never to attend to Geology.' Years later, Darwin was to dedicate the Second Edition of his *Journal* to Lyell in these terms:

> To Charles Lyell FRS, this second edition is dedicated with grateful pleasure, as an acknowledgment that the chief part of whatever scientific merit this journal and the other works of the author may possess has been derived from studying the well-known and admirable *Principles of Geology.*

It is an interesting comment on the efficiency of communication in the age of sail that, when the *Beagle* reached Montevideo, Volume II was sitting there waiting for Darwin. He had supposed that he would not receive Volume III on the voyage, yet we find him writing to Henslow from Valparaiso on 24 July 1834:

> I had deferred reading his third volume till my return, you may guess how much pleasure it gave me; some of his wood-cuts came so exactly into play, that I have only to refer to them, instead of redrawing similar ones.

(For information, Volume I deals with the progress of geology, Volume II with the organic world and Volume III with the history of Tertiary geology).

What made *Principles of Geology* so admirable, and its author so admired? It is a very good example of the *vera causa* work much in vogue at this period. A serious book should start off with the establishment that its subject was a 'true cause', that its subject was worthy of serious consideration and should be capable of being observed in action. Hence Lyell's cumbersome but accurate sub-title does what it says on the tin: *'being an Attempt to explain the Former Changes of the Earth's Surface, by Reference to Causes now in Operation'.*

Principles of Geology comes straight out of the Enlightenment and Scottish common sense philosophy. The earth sciences depend on the witnessing of visible causes, human reason is the tool for their understanding. The book was well-written, well-produced and easily read by the members of the Victorian gentlemanly class at which it was aimed. Lyell said that Murray, the publisher, said:

> There are very few authors, or ever have been, who could write profound science and make a book readable.

Because the book had to be based on observation and experience it was enormous (over 1,400 pages in the First Edition). The Victorians set great store by information and it was packed with examples and pictures, many of them exotic – Italian volcanoes and Pacific coral reefs. There were quotations galore, from five modern languages and the classics. Fieldwork – although Lyell's fieldwork was of the most genteel kind – and observation of the forces of nature at work appealed to the Romanticism of the time. Although traditionalists may have been uneasy about some of the implications, everyone found something of value in the text.

In the chapters giving a *Historical Sketch of the Progress of Geology* he demolished Werner and dealt fully with Hutton and his influence, repeating his own version of Hutton's memorable:

> In the economy of the world, I can find no traces of a beginning, no prospect of an end.

In reminding us that Hutton's views had been questioned because of their association with the revolutionaries in France, he helps us to notice his skill in not bringing to the forefront issues which were later to trouble him, Darwin and society as a whole.

To be grossly simplistic, emerging from the detail was the principle of Uniformitarianism, that 'the present is the key to the past', that the processes operating today are the same processes as have operated since the beginning of time (and there is no need to bring in any others). These geological processes are gradual and therefore require an enormous stretch of time. The notion of the gradual birth and death of species was particularly attractive to Lyell and his whole life could be summed up in the one word – gradualist.

For Lyell the *Principles* brought professional and financial success. The Third Edition, in four small volumes at six shillings (30p) each, brought in another tranche of the reading public and the book eventually ran through 12 editions. For Lyell this meant a continuous process of rewriting and bringing up-to-date, for which he was criticised by Darwin, who thought he should have been doing something more creative. The same might have been said of Lyell's *Elements of Geology* (1838), which ran through seven editions and variants.

HMS *Beagle* returned to Falmouth on 2 October 1836. Even before Darwin's return to England Lyell was keen to meet him. As he wrote to Sedgwick:

> How I long for the return of Darwin! I hope you do not mean to monopolise him at Cambridge.

On 26 December Lyell wrote to Darwin, inviting him to dinner on Monday, 2 December. (This long Letter 335 of the Darwin Correspondence Project also contains the sage advice given below.) Lyell had read Darwin's paper on 'Proofs of recent Elevation on the Coast of Chili' 'with the greatest pleasure' and wished to point out several passages which required explanation. After dinner the Lyells would have one of their:

> small early tea parties, and one or two are to be here, to whom I should like to introduce you, besides a few whom you know already.

This is quite a remarkable letter. Here we have Lyell, writer of the book of the moment, Professor of Geology and President of the Geological Society of London, making the running with a young man, full of promise certainly, but still with slender tangible achievements. Further, he famously goes on to offer Darwin some advice about the future:

> Don't accept any official scientific place, if you can avoid it, and

tell no one that I gave you this advice, as they would all cry out against me as the preacher of anti-patriotic principles. I fought against the calamity of being President as long as I could. All has gone on smoothly, and it has not cost me more time than I anticipated; but my question is, whether the time annihilated by learned bodies (*'par les affaires administratives'*) is balanced by any good they do.

The relationship between Darwin and the Lyells strengthened. Lyell was the first to hear about Darwin's engagement to his cousin Emma and to Emma Darwin wrote, after dining with the Lyells, that it was:

...one of the pleasantest evenings I ever did in my life. Lyell grew quite audacious, at the thoughts of having a married geological companion and proposed going to dine at the Athenaeum together and leaving our wives at home.

Mary Lyell was no Victorian cipher and is always mentioned in the correspondence. The Lyells made trips to Scandinavia, Iceland, Germany, France and America. As Lyell's eyesight deteriorated Mary would read Darwin's letters to him and she began to write Lyell's letters for him. When Darwin congratulated Lyell on his knighthood he concluded: 'Pray give our kindest remembrances to Lady Lyell; how well it sounds!'

Lyell put Darwin up for the Athenaeum and was glad to learn that he enjoyed membership. Lyell announced that his father was delighted with Darwin's *Journal* and there followed an invitation to visit at Kinnordy. How to get there? There were steamboats every Wednesday to Dundee, a passage lasting 36 to 40 hours; railroad four times a day from Dundee to Glamis: 'where the carriage meets you, and brings you in half an hour to Kinnordy.'

The letter concludes: 'Believe me, my dear Darwin, ever most truly yours,' an unusual departure from the usual Victorian conventions.

It was at this period that Darwin persuaded Lyell that he had made a mistake in *Principles*. Lyell had written that coral reefs and atolls formed when mountains rose from the sea. Darwin suggested that the contrary was true, that reefs formed when mountains sank or sea level rose. Lyell generously gave ground and wrote to Darwin in these terms:

I could think of nothing for days after your lesson on coral reefs, but of the tops of submerged continents. It as all true *(sic)*, but do not flatter yourself that you will be believed, till you are going bald, like me with hard work, and vexation at the incredulity of the world.

The friendly relationship between the couples lasted for years. For example, in March 1859 Darwin wrote:

Emma comes up to London for 2–3 days on Friday 6th and she proposes to come and breakfast with Lady Lyell and you on Saturday morning. I have told her that 9½ is your hour, so you need not write.

There were reciprocal visits, as when Darwin invited Lyell to his home at Down:

...to show you my pigeons! Which is the greatest treat, in my opinion, which can be offered to human being.

– pigeons being, of course, the centre of an enormous research project, the outcomes of which were to form a substantial part of the *Origin of Species*. At that weekend in April 1856 Darwin opened up on his theory of natural selection and his ideas on 'the descent of man' – convenient shorthand for the issues around the evolution of *Homo sapiens* and its varied forms. Lyell was the sounding board, but we know that, whatever he said to Darwin, in private he was in mental agony at the prospect of a common descent for all races of humankind and a descent that was related to 'lower species.'

The relationship had begun as that between mentor and promising protégé but Lyell tended to remain in the one place intellectually while Darwin moved on into more controversial areas. Lyell found Darwin disturbing while Darwin found Lyell useful as a sounding board or a Devil's advocate and as a representative of those reluctant to be convinced. Lyell must be given credit for his patience in putting up with Darwin's difficult notions. He continued to have influence and was a master net-worker. It was Lyell who, in 1856, chivvied Darwin into action, action which turned into *Origin of Species*. It was he who persuaded John Murray to publish *Origin of Species*. Lyell read the proofs, a real hack's job totally unsuitable for one of Lyell's social and professional standing and which must have upset Lyell at times.

Over 40 years there was a high degree of coming and going, of soul-searching, doubt and vacillation, with the generation of a vast correspondence. The major areas of controversy were evolution (the changes in individual species over long periods of time), natural selection (the mechanism bringing about evolutionary change), the descent of Man (one species or several?) and transmutation (whether or not one species could change into another). On all these issues Darwin was the innovator while Lyell hung back, could see both sides of the question and was reluctant to put his cards on the table. Yet Lyell was:

> ...the one man in Europe, whose opinion of the general truth of
> a longish argument [Darwin was] always most anxious to hear,

although he kept his ideas on natural selection from him till the last possible moment, and then used him as a piece of litmus to test how the public would react to this strange notion.

According to the first chapter of Genesis, God created every living thing and then said: 'Let us make man in our image'. In other words man was a special creation, in two senses. Lyell saw Darwin attacking man's 'high estate'. and this terrified him. He also had the technical problem of how to revise to keep up with the changing state of knowledge and belief. When Lyell brought out his *Antiquity of Man* in 1863 Darwin cheered it as 'the great book', 4,000 copies going on the first day. However, Hooker had forecast that Lyell would 'have a pretty job to reconcile all his old Geology and Biology to the new state of things'; on closer examination: 'Darwin despaired at Lyell's timidity.' 'Much was said, but so much more was missing.'

Darwin's patience ran out. The Lyells were due for a visit to Down and Darwin prepared to be unpleasant. He was disappointed that Lyell had not come out 'on species, still less on man.' But Lyell had struggled to overturn a view he had held for 30 years and in nine editions of *Principles of Geology*. Darwin had expected support from Lyell and felt so sick that he cancelled the Lyells' visit.

The Lyells visited North America in 1841 and 1845. (Twice later Lyell went back in association with Agassiz.) Out of these visits came two popular travel books – *Travels in North America* (1845) and *A*

Second Visit to the United States of North America (1849). Mary Lyell was quite disturbed by their experiences, especially in the slave South and when they followed the slave route to freedom. In the Episcopalian church in Boston she was distressed at seeing 'seven coloured women' receiving Communion separately. Along the Ohio, four runaway slaves in chains and under armed guard were being dragged back to certain punishment, making her 'feel quite sick'. (Although Charles reassured her that their treatment was little worse than that of deserters being taken back to a regiment.) At Communion in Charleston the cup was offered to the whites before the coloured parishioners, of whose colour she said: 'It does seem very hard and cruel that this badge of serfdom should never be effaced.'

Lyell was against slavery, but on the 'lukewarm' wing of the anti-slavery movement. Hence, his response to this new environment was characteristically equivocal. As a scholar and a gentleman he was popular in the South – among the planters, at least – and, for example, enjoyed a fortnight's hospitality on a plantation with five hundred slaves. There he was the only white man in a Baptist congregation of '600 negroes of various shades.' He knew and approved of churches where 'Negroes sat by permission, with master and slave worshipping together but in separate pews.' This he saw as an immense step in the 'progress towards civilisation.' Compared with many an English villager, many slaves were happier, healthier, more secure and even 'more intelligent'.

The gradualist thought that the blacks could 'only be civilised through slavery.' The system – if humanely managed – would bring the slaves: 'up to the Caucasian standard.' There was a pragmatic argument also: the abolition of slavery would bring about economic and social chaos, in which the ex-slaves would be the worst casualties. Lyell thought the long-term goal of the piecemeal and partial uplift of the blacks was a price worth paying. Darwin knew, of course, that it was not.

Lyell was in the middle of the Darwin–Agassiz relationship and contrived to be friends with both. Although some of the Americans were not too happy about his fieldwork he made many useful contacts. These he passed to Darwin. The Lyells sent him a constant flow of American books. In 1858 Lyell was in the thick of negotiations resulting from Wallace and Darwin simultaneously coming up with evolution papers, negotiations which certainly helped his friend.

The relationship between Lyell and Darwin had many stresses and strains but they retained the greatest respect for each other. Evidence for this is found in a photograph of Darwin's old study at Down House, where Lyell's portrait hung over the fireplace, much as a teenager of today cherishes a poster of a favourite pop star.

Mary Lyell died of typhoid in 1873. She was 12 years younger than her husband, who was heavily dependent on her. Erasmus – Charles' elder brother – broke the news to Emma Darwin, 'leaving her to tell Charles gently.' Hooker described Mary in her coffin. Darwin's feelings, as Desmond and Moore paraphrase the letters:

> welled up, but words failed him. He drafted and redrafted a condolence, settling at last to assure his old friend that 'you are now suffering...the greatest calamity, which a man can endure in the world. God grant that you may have strength to bear your misery.'

Lyell was now almost blind and in poor health. The question of a future life absorbed him and affected his behaviour. Darwin could offer little comfort, any remaining faith he had possessed having been lost with the death of his favourite daughter, Annie, at the age of 10.

Sir Charles Lyell Bart died in 1875 and was buried in Westminster Abbey. He is remembered for Uniformitarianism – 'the present is the key to the past'; dividing the geological record into time periods, mainly based on fossils;
Principles of Geology.

To have left only one of these would have been a major legacy.

Named after him are: craters on the Moon and Mars; Mount Lyell in California; Mount Lyell in Tasmania; Lyell Land in Greenland.

Darwin's comment on his death was quite terse:

> I saw a great deal of Lyell. One of his chief characteristics was his sympathy with the work of others; and I was as much astonished as delighted at the interest which he showed when on my return to England I explained to him my views on coral-reefs.

We are accustomed to Darwin's reticence, but one wonders whether he might not have had more to say than this about forty years of a friendship helpful to him. He chose to highlight Lyell's social skills, perhaps assuming others would need no reminding of his concrete achievements.

He might have mentioned Lyell's generosity of spirit, as when he wrote to Darwin:

I am just revising what I have said in my Anniversary Address, of you and your new Llama, Armadillos, gigantic rodents, and other glorious additions to the Menagerie of that new continent.

Earlier I expressed the opinion that when one thinks of Darwin it is with respect tinged with occasional irritation, but with Lyell the respect is mixed with frustration. 'Poor Lyell, poor Lady Lyell!' wrote Darwin in a letter of 1856, when Lyell was only 59; suggesting that he, too, was uneasy about the Lyells. Lyell peaked early and spent too much time latterly – in Darwin's view – revising and editing and networking. Yet it was Lyell who had advised Darwin against committees! It may be that his creativity had died; perhaps the failing eyesight and the indignity of having to be helped were factors. Whatever the cause there is no doubt that the relationship changed over the years as Lyell marked time while Darwin raced ahead with his latest notion, after arriving at it by the long way round.

Both were born in easy circumstances and could be 'gentleman naturalists' all their long lives. I doubt if Lyell was jealous of Darwin, but there must have been a twinge of envy from time to time. The Lyells were childless, while Darwin had a large family and a rich family life. Lyell was hampered by his birth and upbringing, which made it hard for him to communicate with lesser mortals. Although Darwin could be almost a recluse, he could also share interests and mix with ordinary people like farmers and pigeon fanciers. Despite his early experience at Edinburgh he enjoyed the messier tasks of research, while Lyell was always reluctant to get his hands dirty.

Darwin was essentially a happy man, happy in his home, happy in his work, despite the repeated illnesses. It is unlikely that Lyell was happy, latterly. There were too many minuses in his life.

Even in death there was an unsatisfactory angle. It was intended that Darwin should be buried next to Lyell, in Westminster Abbey, close in death as they had been in life, but in the event he was laid to rest in even better company, below the monument to Newton and next to Sir John Herschel, the great astronomer, whom Darwin had visited in South Africa.

CHAPTER SIX

The Riddle of Glen Roy

A JOURNEY FROM INVERNESS to Newtonmore or Dalwhinnie along the A9, then via the A86 to Spean Bridge, and back to Inverness along the Great Glen using the A82, follows the sides of a giant triangle whose sides are, respectively, 46 (or 56), 37 and 56 miles. Within this triangle is a vast area almost without human habitation. Most of it is high moorland with 11 separate mountains over 3,000 feet (914.4 metres) lining the southern flank. Three fine rivers, the Nairn, the Findhorn and the Spey drain north-eastward to the Moray Firth. Upper Lochaber, in the south-west corner, is drained by the Spean, which has two substantial tributaries, the Gloy and the Roy. The only through road was General Wade's military road from Ruthven Barracks on Speyside over the Corrieyairick Pass at 2,768 feet to Fort Augustus at the south end of Loch Ness. Otherwise, the only roads run a few miles up some of the valleys before petering out.

The key to Glen Roy is Roy Bridge, which has a station on the West Highland Railway, two hotels, one old, one newish, a post office, a village shop ('the last for 28 miles') and St Margaret's Catholic Church.

Upper Lochaber was one of the parts of the Highlands the Reformation did not reach and which supported the Jacobites. Just up the glen from the village is a cairn with a plaque:

The Battle of Mulroy
4 August 1688
On the hill opposite The Macdonnells of Keppoch defeated the
Mackintoshes in the last inter-clan battle fought in Scotland.

Later the same year in Glen Roy, Graham of Claverhouse and Cameron of Locheil joined forces for the campaign that ended with their victory at Killiecrankie (1689), the death of Claverhouse and the collapse of the uprising.

Earlier, in what is usually called the English Civil War, James Graham, Marquis of Montrose, pulled off an extraordinary military achievement.

Having ravaged Argyll early in 1645, he was being pursued north along the Great Glen, only to find his way blocked (at what was later called Fort Augustus) by another Covenanting force. Undaunted, and acting on the intelligence and advice of Ian Lom, The Bard of Keppoch, on 31 January he led his men on the toughest march in the military history of Scotland.

Over the maze of snow-covered mountains around the headwaters of the Spey, down Glen Roy and round the lower slopes of Ben Nevis the Royalist army struggled, to reach Inverlochy on 2 February. Surprise was complete, half of the Covenanting army was slaughtered and Campbell of Argyll lost his reputation by sitting out the battle in his galley and allowing himself to be rowed away while his loyal clansmen were massacred.

Straight lines, especially straight lines in threes several miles long, are not common in nature and the early inhabitants found it difficult to account for what became known as the Parallel Roads of Glen Roy. The ministers who wrote the Old and New Statistical Accounts of the parish of Kilmonivaig demonstrate how ideas were changing around the beginning of the 19th century. For Mr Thomas Ross in 1793 the Parallel Roads were:

> one of the most stupendous monuments of human industry, and which well deserve the attention of the antiquary.

After an accurate description he says that there is nothing left on record regarding their origin and 'can only mention the common traditions concerning them.' One was that they were made by the kings of Scotland for them to hunt when in residence at Inverlochy Castle. So vast an undertaking could not be effected by any vassal or nobleman, however powerful. The Great Hall of Stirling Castle was probably the largest single construction of any Scottish king. The technical challenge of building one road, far less three, makes the idea of a royal building work in Glen Roy ludicrous.

Locally the roads were known as *Fingalian roads*. Fingal, he of Mendelssohn's cave, built a causeway to Ulster, to the Giant's Causeway, then tore it up when he crossed it to find Finn McCool posing as a baby. The heroes of Fingal made the Parallel Roads for hunting. The glen was heavily forested and avenues were made to pursue the deer. Palisades were erected to steer them into a field called *Dalnafealg* (hunting dale) where they were killed. Stakes were found driven into the sides of the road – so it must have been true!

With the pacification of the Highlands and the beginning of tourism such a strange natural phenomenon became a must for the curious traveller. The literati came to gaze at the sublime savagery of the landscape and their simple wonder became speculation as serious members of the Enlightenment studied these ancient traces – of what?

In view of one's admiration for John Playfair it gives one no pleasure to record that:

> So lately as 1816, Mr Playfair sent a letter to the Royal Society of Edinburgh, setting them down as aqueducts for artificial irrigation, like those he had seen in the Valais near Brig.

As if the struggling crofters of the Western Highlands required any more water than was generously provided by the forces of nature!

The Rev John McIntyre (1843) has two pages, starting thus:

> Parallel roads of Glenroy
> The following account of these celebrated indented lines is taken from the Edinburgh Philosophical Journal, Vol xxvii.

After the description he quotes Dr McCulloch and Sir Thomas Dick Lauder's solution to the problem. Essentially Glen Roy, Glen Spean and Glen Gloy each had its own loch, held back by a barrier of loose stones and earth. The Glen Roy barrier gave way partially and the waters rushed out in two phases, three lake terraces being the result. The account concludes:

> Mr Darwin has lately proposed another theory: that the terraces are sea-beaches, formed at the period when the now elevated land constituted a low and level bay of the ocean, and that the periodical elevation of this land gave time for the formation of two or three littoral indentations. Mr Darwin illustrates his theory by analogous phenomena in Peru.

Sir Thomas Dick Lauder, 7th Baronet of Fountainhall (1784–1848) was a good all-rounder who, according to *Collins Encyclopaedia of Scotland* (1994):

> could make his way in the world as a player, or a ballad singer, or a street fiddler, or a geologist. Or a civil engineer, or a surveyor, as easily and eminently as an artist or a layer out of ground.

After military service he became Secretary to three important national bodies, the Board of Manufactures and Fisheries in Scotland, the Board of British White Fishery and the Royal Institution for the Encouragement of the Fine Arts. He was active in organising public support for the 1832 Reform Bill. He wrote novels and travel books and was asked by Queen Victoria to write the official history of her 1843 Royal Progress in Scotland. If he is remembered today it is subliminally in one of Edinburgh's finer Victorian suburbs. The Grange of St Giles was acquired by William Dick in 1631 and the Dick Lauder family feued it out in the 19th century. Thus we have Grange Road, Court, Loan and Terrace, Fountainhall Road, Relugas Road, Dalrymple Crescent, Dick Place, Lauder Road, Cumin Place, Seton Place, Findhorn Place, commemorating family members or properties.

Dick Lauder's *An Account of the Great Floods in Morayshire in 1829 in the Province of Moray and adjoining Districts* was published in 1830, a truly remarkable achievement. Torrential rain and the fact that so much farmland had been 'improved', resulting in a swift run-off, combined to give rise to spectacular flooding in north-east Scotland. Bridges and mills were swept away and fertile farmland inundated. So spectacular was the flood that it passed into folk memory, witness the following:

> An' the Duke an's dother shook his han' an' speirt aboot his kin.
> 'Old family, yes: here sin' the flood,' I smairtly chippit in.
> (Fiech! Noah's? Na – We'd ane wirsels, ye ken, in '29.)
> (Mary Symon, *The Glen's Muster-Roll: The Dominie Loquitur*)

Dick Lauder showed great enterprise and energy in following up the flood, interviewing witnesses and inspecting damage.

It is not surprising that such an inquisitive soul should be the first to investigate the origin of the Parallel Roads, which he did in 1818, in a paper to the Royal Society of Edinburgh 'The Parallel Roads of Glenroy'. His main qualification for investigating the Parallel Roads was a love of country and a quick, lively mind.

The local people Darwin met in Glen Roy in 1839 were Gaelic-speaking. They seem to have been short on imagination in naming their local landmarks. Closing the view at the head of the main glen are two Carn Deargs (red cairns) and a Carn Dearg Beag (small red cairn). There is another Carn Dearg on the eastern side of the upper glen. Lower down are two Leana Mhors (big meadows), one on either side of the river. The crofting township of Bohuntine is *both chundainn* – the house at the confluence – which describes its original site well enough. Despite the name, nearby Bohuntineville was not a new foundation set up to resettle soldiers after Waterloo. In 1568 the settlement was *Bohintene-villie*, the suffix *bhaile* being Gaelic for village.

Evidence of the clash of cultures is found in a large stone, like a milestone, at the roadside. A *bocan* or spectre of ill-repute terrorised the local people until, in 1770, Mass was offered up on a large stone in the bed of the stream the hobgoblin haunted. Around 1880 the stone was broken by roadmakers. Young MacPherson, a native of Glen Roy, rescued half of the great stone, set it up as a memorial and cut into the top a chalice, a wafer of bread and the letters 'IHS'.

Probably more conducive to confusion than the naming of places was the lack of a good base map for Darwin to work from. An investigation of 'parallel roads' was bound to require a knowledge of precise altitudes and levels, yet the first Six-Inch Ordnance Survey map of the area was not surveyed until 1870.

The One-Inch map of 1873 was the first to have contours, essential for showing the shape of the land. Unfortunately, the vertical interval was 250 feet, so that delineation of land form was rather crude. What is interesting and makes this Sheet 63 unique is a table of Levels of Parallel Roads in the bottom left margin. For each Parallel Road – one in Glen Gloy, three in Glen Roy, one in Glen Spean – three values are given: Highest, Lowest and Average. For each Road also is given the height of the col out of which the temporary loch drained.

Underneath is a key to the ice barriers marked on the map – A to B, C to D, E to F, and a note of Sketches marked on the map by numbers 1 to 6. On the corresponding modern Explorer 400 1/25000 map of 2001 none of this supplementary information is given.

The observant traveller will have noted, on prominent viewpoints, small concrete pillars each with a metal base plate on top. These are the triangulation stations from the basic Ordnance Survey of Great Britain. Their positions and altitudes are known to a high degree of accuracy. Scattered around, on prominent buildings, bridges, large boulders and the like, are metal studs or the Government broad arrow. These spot heights and bench marks are correct to 0.1 of a foot, or the metric equivalent.

For the 1898 OS map of Glen Roy it was clear that special attention had obviously been paid to the Parallel Roads. Along each road is a succession of spot heights, to the nearest foot, and bench marks. On the western side of the glen a series of 17 bench marks is recorded, making it possible to draw an accurate cross-section.

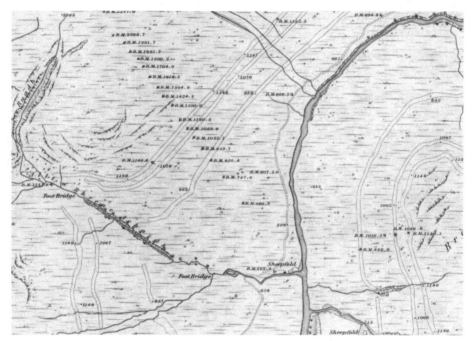

FIG 12: The Parallel Roads in 1898
(*Ordnance Survey Six-Inch map*)

Modern confusion is not helped by *Field Geology in the British Isles* (1983) which carries out the remarkable feat of transferring the *Allt Glass Dhoire* – a big burn – from the eastern to the western side of Glen Roy! With hindsight it is difficult to imagine the confusion Darwin must have felt as he was driven up the glen for the first time. The three Parallel Roads are absolutely clear high up on both sides of the glen for several miles. Yet, when one climbs the mountainside, they become less apparent. The terraces are not flat, they slope, but at a less steep angle than the hillside. Although they are former beaches 10 to 30 metres wide, there is not much sign of boulders or sand, merely a broad strip even wetter than the sodden hillside. The roads have been cut by later streams, which have deposited the eroded material in fans on the valley floor.

FIG 13: Upper Glen Roy, the two higher Parallel Roads

Around Braeroy Lodge, where the lowest Road approaches the level of the river, is an area of great complexity where the (present-day) Turret joins the upper Roy. Vast amounts of water have been sloshing around here at various times, with huge deposits of sand, gravel and larger boulders. Deltas were deposited around the lake edges. Their top surfaces are usually horizontal in one sense and gently sloping in another. While masses of stagnant ice still occupied the valley floor meltwater washed in masses of fluvio-glacial material which accumulated between the ice and the valley wall. When the ice melted the resulting kame terraces were left with a steep face towards the river and a flattish top lining the valley sides, gently sloping downstream. Like most other big Scottish rivers, the Roy filled parts of its valley with sediment, which it is now re-excavating, creating flat-topped river terraces. Since Jamieson provided his solution in 1863 we have had the theory of relativity, nuclear fission and space travel yet Sissons could say in *The Evolution of Scotland's Scenery* (1967):

certain problems remain to be solved and much basic mapping of the fluvoglacial landforms has yet to be done.

Without a decent map, this area must have seemed utter chaos to Darwin on that first visit, with horizontals and near-horizontals going in all directions, sometimes running into each other and sometimes cutting across others. Darwin was, however, spared another distraction obvious to today's observer. Glen Spean has its share of former lake beaches and high on its southern side a marked horizontal runs for several miles. This is the track of the light railway built by the British Aluminium Company to service its dam at Loch Treig.

Some personal reminiscence will complete this setting of the scene of Darwin's 'eight good days'. I first visited Glen Roy in the late 1940s, before the narrow, twisting road was tarred. Our family toured the Highlands every summer. One year I was determined to see the Parallel Roads for myself and persuaded a reluctant father to take me to the spot where there is now a car park and a viewpoint. We admired the view and wondered at these strange straight lines on the mountain sides. Then I climbed up to inspect the Roads themselves. I have forgotten what I expected to see, but I know I was disappointed. For such a prominent feature the close-up is an anti-climax.

Looking up the glen, I was never so terrified in my life. While I was absorbed in what was under my feet a huge storm had gathered and was now heading down the valley, straight at me! I had never before seen anything as big and black and filthy as the boiling mass of cloud which was tearing down, channelled by the steep valley sides. I cantered down to the car at a dangerous pace, almost making it to safety. Instead I was overwhelmed by a ferocious mass of hail and sleet, delivered with tremendous force and accompanied by crashing thunder and the occasional flash of lightning.

Many years later I felt it necessary to climb the Leana Mhor east of the Roy. I left my car high above the river, on the west side, and followed an old road down to the river gorge at Cranachan Bridge – to find that the bridge existed on the map but not in reality. The Roy is a superb canoeing river – one of the best in Scotland – and a canoeist, assembling his gear, volunteered to take me across. Across that boiling hell of water and rock? And how would I get back, assuming I survived the first crossing?

So it was back to Roy Bridge and up the public road to Bohenie, from which the Forestry Commission had made one of their access roads. It went round a hill, down into a valley, across a big burn – the *Allt Glass Dhoire* mentioned above – up through a big, mature plantation and along the level hillside to a point opposite the Cranachan bridge but about 120 metres higher up and a good stepping-off point for Leana Mhor, which was good compensation for the frustrating experience of an hour earlier. Even better was to find out from the map that I had driven for a full kilometre along the lowest of the Parallel Roads and that I might even be the first person to drive along one of the Parallel Roads for pleasure!

Before turning to Darwin's expedition it would be helpful to summarise what we now think really happened in and around Glen Roy in the closing phases of the most recent glaciation.

FIG 14: Ice-dammed lakes at time of maximal ice extent

About 13,000 years ago the Loch Lomond Readvance took place, the most recent spectacular incident in our glacial story. West of Lochaber, in an area of high rainfall, high snowfall and high mountains, the ice accumulated and pushed its way eastwards, filling the lower ground around Loch Lochy, Spean Bridge and Glen Spean, blocking existing valleys and forming lakes. The lakes remained at this level for some considerable time, long enough for the normal processes of lakeside erosion and deposition to form the parallel road in Glen Gloy at 355 metres and the highest parallel road in Glen Roy at 350 metres. The Glen Gloy lake overflowed into the Glen Roy lake at 3, while the latter overflowed into the upper reaches of the Spey at 3. (See FIG 14. At the same time the loch in Glen Spean also overflowed at 3, to join the Spey just off the map.)

The most recent explanation of the three levels is that the ice advanced in three stages, with long spells of quiescence between when the lakes were eroding their shores. The first advance created a barrier behind which the lake creating the lowest parallel road formed at 261 metres. This lake filled Glen Roy and Glen Spean and found an outlet to the upper Spey at 1. The Glen Spean lake was about 60 metres deep, but the other two were real Highland glacial lakes – the Glen Roy lake was some 200 metres deep and that in Glen Gloy 170 metres in depth.

The second advance created the lake for the second parallel road in Glen Roy at 326 metres. The Glen Spean and Glen Roy lakes were now separate and at different levels. The Glen Roy overspill drained through a col into Glen Spean at 2 on the sketch map. From time to time, the ice dam failed and the lake waters escaped in huge floods, creating the spectacular gorge of the Spean (4). Darwin described the feature thus:

> On Tombhran a great gorge which is impassable, and where the rock is bare and shattered, has been deeply cut into.

Such floods are known in Iceland as *jökulhlaups* – glacier bursts. Another example of the present being the key to the past.

Such is the sequence described on the interpretation board in Glen Roy and generally accepted since about 1970. I have to say, however, that a week before this was written I revisited Glen Roy and had doubts about this sequence. Jamieson (1829–1913) in 1863 put forward an interpretation based on the situation as in FIG 14 being the first stage, with the two lower roads being formed as the ice barrier thinned and receded, and, to me, this seems to fit the evidence.

Darwin did not wander into Glen Roy like a *tabula rasa*, laid back and waiting for impressions to wash over him. In Cambridge University Library is a single sheet of paper, watermarked 1837, and containing 16 numbered notes – 'Chief points to be attended to.' Here are a few extracts, with comments.

Darwin had clearly studied Dick Lauder and MacCulloch's papers – were the shelves due to accumulation (MacCulloch) or corroding (Dick Lauder)?

'Organic remains. *Balani. Serpula* – calcareous matter.' Darwin was to look for evidence of marine conditions.

'Relative height of 2nd shelf and Loch Spey' – overflow cols had not been found or agreed by Dick Lauder and MacCulloch.

'The relative preservation of the shelves' – would have a bearing on the length of the pauses between changes in lake levels.

'Examine Tom-na-fersit and entrance of Loch Treig for *Balani* and smooth waterworn rocks, also Barnacles on transported blocks.'

Why the barnacles? Because the accumulation of shells would be proof that the roads were sea beaches. In the event, no shells were found, whereupon Darwin produced an ingenious argument that lack of marine shells was a proof of the marine origin of the beaches!

Darwin had been overwhelmed by his experiences in Chile and was to look for corroboration of his notion that the roads were sea beaches subjected to a lengthy process of crustal elevation. There is every evidence from the completed paper that Darwin covered these points and many more in a frenzy of activity over 'eight good days' – although on one day he was ill and could not venture into one of the areas he wished to study.

'Observations on the Parallel Roads of Glen Roy, and of other parts of Lochaber in Scotland, with an attempt to prove that they are of marine origin' may not have been a snappy title, but it certainly told the reader what to expect. Completed on 6 September 1838, submitted on 17 January 1839 and read on 7 February, it comprises 42 pages, with four line drawings and an attractive base map using hachures to show the mountains, with the terraces added. Mr Albert Way (1805–74) lent Darwin a drawing of Glen Roy, ('It very faithfully represents the general appearance of Glen Roy.') which was lithographed and added to the paper. Way and Darwin had been students together at Cambridge. Way is best remembered for his caricature of Darwin astride a beetle.

The paper is divided into sections, as follows.

'Section VII – On the erratic boulders of Lochaber', is the shortest section
and, perhaps, the easiest to deal with. All over the surface of the study
area are sizeable boulders, generally granite, which have not been derived
from the parent rock but have been brought in from some distance.
These erratics were found as high as 2,200 feet. The granitic area from
which the 'Ben Erin' erratics came is 920 feet below their present location.
Darwin offered two means by which they could have been brought in, 'by

some overwhelming debacle' or by being frozen into drifting icebergs which released the boulders as they melted. There are no traces of the actions of the waters of such a debacle while – for icebergs to be floating above the present-day hilltops – huge dams and lakes would have been necessary. No traces of such have been found. Yet Darwin manages to reject the first explanation and use the second as proof of enormous amounts of recent uplift of the land. And in his next section he describes striations and other features, which we would recognise as the work of ice, as the result of water action.

In his fieldwork Darwin certainly covered the ground, up to over 2,000 feet, checking on his predecessors – who differed on some points – and seeking out new critical locations. There is a great deal to be said about the mountain barometer ('which stood at the same thousandth of an inch on the two stations'), his main means of measuring altitude. Checking on his fieldwork is only possible in a few named locations, most of his evidence being only vaguely located – no grid references or GPS positioning then!

Darwin brought to the task his own experience and observation in South America – if a thousand miles of Chile coastline could be heaved up by four feet in one night as lately as 1822 (as reported by Chambers in *Vestiges of Creation*) who knows what might have happened in Glen Roy! In addition, in a manner that was to become characteristic of his later big projects, he cast his net wide in the search for evidence.

Lyell provided relevant information based on his observations in Sweden and on the Angus coast. 'In a letter from a steamboat on the Rhine' he described the movement of erratics without using the word:

> The blocks of red syenitic granite, which I hammered away at in Norway...have been carried with small gravel of the same, by ice of course, over the south of Norway, and thence down the south-west of Sweden, and all over Jutland and Holstein down to the Elbe, from whence they come to the Weser, and so to this or near this.

Note – 'by ice, of course.'

Lyell also passed on useful information about terraces in Strathmore from Mr Blackadder, a civil engineer. Roderick Murchison, later Director-General of the Geological Survey of Great Britain, sparked off a search for recent sea shells in Shropshire and Staffordshire. Darwin was no intellectual snob and was happy to report that he had been informed by an intelligent quarryman that he had observed many broken sea-shells in a gravel-pit 18 miles from the nearest sea-coast. Hillwalkers know that the watershed between two river systems is often not a high ridge but a level, and often broad 'land-strait', to use Darwin's term. It was 'an intelligent shepherd' who accompanied Darwin and who remarked that this form of the land was common wherever the waters in this mountainous country divided, whereupon Darwin observed several instances of it.

In Scotland, glaciers, ice and its after-effects were very much au courant as a topic. All that was needed was a big name to confirm what many suspected to be true, and that big name turned up in 1840.

The next distinguished visitor to Glen Roy was Louis Agassiz (1807–73), probably the most respected geologist in the world in 1840 and certainly the top man on fossil fish. He was brought to Scotland, lecturing in Glasgow before touring the Highlands, ending up in Edinburgh. In Glen Roy he had no difficulty in recognising the evidence for ice-dammed lakes, which were common enough in the Alps, where he had a research station on the Unteraar Glacier. From Fort Augustus he wrote to Professor Jameson, Darwin's *bête noire*, announcing his discovery. Charles MacLaren of *The Scotsman* was also a geologist so that on 7 October 1840 the Ice Age was first announced to the general public under the headline:

> Discovery of former glaciers in Scotland, especially in the Highlands, by Professor Agassiz.

In Edinburgh he was famously taken to Blackford Glen, where he stated boldly: 'This is the work of the ice.' (Sadly, it is no longer possible to see what Agassiz saw. The Agassiz Rock was protected by a fence. When it disappeared the rock became the scene for 'sausage sizzles' by the Brownies and, later, for more harmful pursuits, destroying all the evidence.)

There had been rumblings, particularly in Scotland, about a glacial episode in the past – but this was different. Agassiz was the greatest authority in the world and his easy recognition of the previous existence of glaciers and ice-dammed lakes became the new orthodoxy after he delivered his findings at the Geological Society on 4 November.

Darwin had returned from Glen Roy well pleased with himself: 'My Scotch expedition answered brilliantly.' His paper on Glen Roy 'crowned the series on global elevation', and clinched his fellowship of the Royal Society.

Agassiz's intuitive pronouncement was therefore quite a blow for Darwin. His first major scientific paper was, at the very least, in question. Darwin had postulated arms of the sea lifted several hundred feet into the air, Agassiz saw a dam of ice with a succession of lakes at lower levels. Desmond and Moore say:

> Agassiz's icy catastrophism made Darwin shiver, gentle rising and subsidence of the land was the key.

Raised sea-beaches or ice-dammed lakes, which was the greater catastrophe? Of a second order supporter of Agassiz, Darwin said: 'I think his Glen Roy theory more utterly impossible than words can express.' Unfortunately for Darwin, others put flesh on Agassiz's bones and to Hooker he wrote:

> ...having had to think and write too much about Glen Roy (an audacious son of dog [sic] having attacked my theory) which made me horribly sick.

On 9 March 1841 Darwin wrote to Lyell defending his own interpretation against the glacial theory. Yet he could still say, anent Agassiz's book *Etudes sur les glaciers*, 'What a capital book Agassiz's is.' Darwin was still convinced he was right. At Southampton he still thought that 'there was never a more futile theory' than Agassiz's glacial lakes, 'But the Swiss savant's ice sheets were sweeping all before them.'

Agassiz was 'a good genial fellow', 'his bonhomie seemed inexhaustible,' and there is no evidence that he held any personal animus against Darwin. He enjoyed being a celebrity and displayed a natural bumptiousness at showing off his knowledge, along with the missionary's satisfaction at making converts. His association with Darwin began in September 1846, at the Southampton meeting of the British Association for the Advancement of Science. Darwin was on the brink of his eight-year study of barnacles and Agassiz spoke on the necessity for such a study. Immediately afterwards Lyell took Agassiz to Liverpool to set off for a new life in the United States, which brought, in succession, the Chair of Natural History at Harvard, much solid achievement in science, a new wife and American citizenship. He also discovered a horror of and antipathy towards black people. In American society he was fêted and admired, developing a special affinity with the charming slave-owners of the South and finding that some aspects of slavery were quite acceptable.

Darwin and Agassiz kept in contact, although their ideas diverged. Agassiz shipped off a crate of barnacles for Darwin to work on. Two weeks before the launch of *Origin of Species,* a specimen copy was sent off to Agassiz (not sent, said Darwin, 'in a spirit of defiance or bravado.')

Darwin believed in evolution and that *Homo sapiens* was a species that had differentiated with time into a number of races. Agassiz came to believe in multiple creations and polygenism – that there were eight distinct species of men. Both of these ideas appealed to the South and provided some sort of scientific justification for the practice of slavery.

To me it is almost beyond belief that Agassiz could at the same time say that black and white were separate species and could not therefore interbreed, and look around at the streets and cotton fields filled with mulattos, sambos, 'high yallers', quadroons and octaroons. Compared with this astigmatism Darwin's confusion over barnacles and beaches seems quite trivial.

Darwin, of course, came from a family of anti-slavery activists. Twice he was the grandson of leading abolitionists – Erasmus Darwin and Josiah Wedgwood, who bankrolled the abolitionist cause. His three elder sisters were active humanitarians and he married Emma, one of four humanitarian Wedgwood girls. Although Darwin did not campaign openly against American slavery there is no doubt that the gap between him and Agassiz widened on more than scientific grounds.

On an Agassiz essay of 1855 on aboriginal men Darwin said: 'How false...what forced reasoning.' On homelands 'determined by the will of the Creator' he scribbled down: 'Oh for shame Agassiz.' To Asa Gray, a botanist colleague of Agassiz at Harvard, Darwin let off steam – Agassiz's 'superficiality and wretched reasoning powers' disgusted him. Agassiz arrogantly got out of tight corners by saying: 'Nature never lied.' Of course, only Agassiz understood Nature. 'Agassiz's foolish notion' of a creation every time the earth needed 'a new form of lizard' – or a new human race – was subverted. With Gray, Darwin agreed that Agassiz was great – 'great in taking the wrong view.'

During the American Civil War Agassiz was still at Harvard, where he sought federal regulation to stop interracial crossing. He was writing 'very maundering geology and zoology' and would not 'be of any more use to natural history.' Darwin's reaction was:

> I must say I enjoy anything which riles Agassiz. He seems to grow bigoted with increasing years.

Was Darwin still sore at the contradiction of his Glen Roy solution or were the issues between the two savants more fundamental than that? When he came to write his *Autobiography* he realised that his approach to Glen Roy was fundamentally wrong. Instead of applying the Baconian method of accumulating observations, analysing them and producing hypotheses to be tested, he came fresh from the *Beagle* and South American earthquakes and tried to make the Highland landscape fit his preconceptions.

Many years after this incident he was to write:

> During these two years I took several short excursions as a relaxation, and one longer to the parallel roads of Glen Roy, an account of which was published in the Philosophical Transactions. This paper was a great failure, and I am ashamed of it. Having been deeply impressed with what I had seen of the elevation of the land in South America, I attributed the parallel lines to the action of the sea; but I had to give up this view when Agassiz propounded his glacier-lake theory. Because no other explanation was possible under our then state of knowledge, I argued in favour of sea-action; and my error has been a good lesson to me never to trust in science to the principle of exclusion.

Support for Darwin came from an unexpected direction. Robert Chambers, four years after the anonymous publication of *Vestiges of Creation,* paid two visits to Glen Roy. The reception of *Vestiges* had persuaded him that he had to prove himself more than a hack journalist by taking on a big project, which came into the public domain as *Ancient Sea Margins* (1848). Like Darwin and his barnacles, this would be his 'passport to acceptance.' Darwin wrote him a long letter of advice, in which he asked Chambers if he (Darwin) might call on him and also showed a weakening of resolution:

...if the roads were formed by a Lake of any kind, I believe it must have been an ice lake.

In another letter he said: 'In the first two days I was a convert to the lacustrine theory' but features of the topography convinced him that his marine theory was correct.

Ancient Sea Margins came out in 1848, and included 42 pages on Lochaber. Chambers took a definite anti-Agassiz line. The book is a real *tour de force*. The title page proudly proclaims that Robert Chambers is a Fellow of the Royal Society of Edinburgh. There are over 200 pages of detailed observation and descriptions, preceded by General Descriptions and Facts and followed by General Observations and examples from Switzerland, Scandinavia and North America. He really pulled out all the stops in Glen Roy, with pages of detailed measurements and observations, some:

> According to a levelling survey executed for the first time at my request, by William Paterson, under the directions of Joseph Mitchell Esq, civil engineer, Inverness, whose conduct throughout my inquiries has been most obliging.

FIG 15: Glen Roy in the time of Chambers (*Ancient Sea Margins*)

True to his *Vestiges* form, Chambers hits us at the very beginning:

> Taking observed facts for our data, we know that there was a time subsequent to the completion of the rock formations, when this island (not to speak of other parts of the earth) was submerged to the height of at least 1,700 feet. The proofs lie plain and palpable before our eyes, in the soft detrital masses, mixed in many places with marine shells, which overlie the hardened

formations, reaching in some places to that height above the present sea-level.

Unfortunately, he now invoked Roderick Murchison, President of the Geological Society, who correctly deduced the Irish origins of chalks, flints and shells found high on the Moel Tryfan in north Wales, but mistakenly ascribed their means of transport there as having been the result of the action of the sea.

For Glen Roy Chambers concluded:

> It thus appears as in the highest degree probable that the Parallel Roads of Glen Roy, together with other similar or only slightly diverse markings in the same district, are the memorials of these glens having once been the beds of arms of the sea, exactly like those of Loch Hourn, Lochnanuagh, and the many others, which at this day serrate the western coast of Inverness-shire.

Chambers's book is admirable in so many ways, yet it suffers because it attempts to find one explanation for all terraces, whatever their origin and even their location. One can think of at least four separate ways in which terraces are formed and the majority of upland terraces, certainly in Scotland, are the result of the deposition of fluvio-glacial materials by vigorous meltwaters, rather than of erosion and deposition by relatively quiescent bodies of water, whether lochs or arms of the sea.

Because the authorship was known, it was easy to mount an attack *ad hominem* and *Ancient Sea Margins* was labelled as by an 'essayist of the middle class', the fieldwork dismissed as 'puerilities about terraces.'

Lyell, cautious but correct, advised caution in its interpretation.

Darwin, not by any means a disinterested party, was full of praise for Chambers:

> I am delighted to hear what progress your Book has made; I had no idea that you were going to publish so grand an affair as 30 engravings sounds like. I am glad you are prepared to fight stoutly with the sceptical geologists.

Yet this was the same Darwin who had, the year before, at Oxford, slated The Unknown's 'poverty of intellect' and dismissed *Vestiges* as a 'literary curiosity', although his complimentary copy must have cleared up the authorial mystery for him.

Thomas Jamieson (1829–1913) was no gilded amateur but one of the leading artisan scientists of his generation, a principal figure in the decoding of our glacial story. He established the basic sequence of glaciation and sea-level change in Scotland and recognised the role of ice sheets in eroding the landscape. In 1865 he put forward the concept of isostasy, the rising of the land after the great mass of ice which covered it had melted. Ironically, the Parallel Roads, like all of Scotland, have experienced isostatic uplift – but nothing like the catastrophic uplift that Darwin had postulated.

Jamieson kept in touch with the authorities on the Parallel Roads. On 24 March 1862 he wrote to Darwin, asking him to show the letter to 'Sir C Lyell', 'as it wd save me writing it over again.' He had already written to Robert Chambers and David Milne-Home, 'but failed to elicit anything certain on the subject.' The subject is his final confirmation that the level of the lowermost Road matches exactly the supposed outlet eastwards towards the Spey – confirmed by the accurate levelling of the Ordnance Survey, then in progress.

As we have seen, Jamieson's solution to the riddle proved satisfactory for over a century and has only been modified in detail in recent years.

Darwin did not like being wrong in public and it may well have been that the Glen Roy experience reinforced his tendency to procrastinate until he was absolutely sure he was correct before launching into print. In fact, the deteriorating relationship with Agassiz was due, in part at least, to the fact that the *Origin of Species* was in gestation at the same time as Agassiz was winning over an audience in both the USA and Britain to his versions of creationism and polygenism. While Darwin was honing his material, grizzling over his mistakes and seeking reassurance before delivering his crushing blow, Agassiz was out there, cheerfully making converts.

Darwin's reaction was to make a systematic approach in one easily defined field in order to establish himself as a serious scientist. Barnacles presented a neat and definite challenge which he would be able to master in a few months. In the event, the project grew and grew till it occupied eight years of his life, satisfying all that could have been expected from him.

As far as Glen Roy was concerned, however, a lesser man than

Darwin might have taken comfort in what Thomas Alva Edison was to say at the end of the century: 'The man who never made a mistake never made anything.'

CHAPTER SEVEN

The Anatomist and the Alienist

THE EXPRESSION OF THE Emotions in Men and Animals was published in November 1872, following hard on the heels of *The Origin of Species* (1869) and *The Descent of Man* (1871). Written in four months, it had been long in gestation. Darwin claimed that booksellers subscribed to 5,267 copies on the day of publication, making *The Expression of Emotions* his first-day bestseller. Darwin's royalties amounted to over 1,000 guineas. A posthumous second edition appeared in 1890.

Patently, *The Expression of Emotions* was a great success in its time – 'tickling a shocked, blushing, eyebrow-raising Victorian generation' – but can we take seriously something written 130 years ago in ignorance of Mendel's work in his Austrian monastery and long before the discovery of 'the selfish gene', a neat term introduced in 1976?[7]

The Expression of Emotions is still worth reading because it is interesting and stimulating. It was an early attempt to describe and explain some of the intangibles behind human (and animal) behaviour. It illustrates how Darwin handled one of his big projects. It was one of the first books to use photography for more than decorative purposes and the assembly of the components of the book is an absorbing technical study. Above all, it illustrates Darwin's tenacity in using one of his peripheral Edinburgh interests and bringing it into the public domain 40-plus years later.

The story begins with the Plinian Society of the University of Edinburgh or, before that, with the publication by Charles (later Sir Charles) Bell of *The Anatomy and Philosophy of Expression*. As Darwin wrote, many years later, probably thinking of the 3rd edition of 1844:

> I read Sir C. Bell's admirable work on Expression, and this greatly increased the interest which I felt in the subject, though I could not at all agree with his belief that various muscles had been specially created for the sake of expression. From this time forward I occasionally attended to the subject, both with respect to man and our domestic animals.

As we have seen, the Plinian Society was a major extra-curricular influence on Darwin's development at Edinburgh. A leading figure in that circle was William Alexander Frances Browne (1805–85). He was one of the three Presidents of the Society who proposed Darwin for membership, and presumably supported his election to the Council of the Society. Older than Darwin, he was another positive influence during his student days. Browne was born in Stirling and became LRCS in 1826. He attended the university classes of Chemistry and Practice of Physic in 1826–27, using the Plinian Society as an outlet for a paper refuting Bell's ideas. He visited the asylums of Paris and returned to Stirling to practise. In 1834 he was appointed Medical Superintendent of the Royal Asylum at Montrose. Five years later he became the first Superintendent of the newly founded Crichton Institution at Dumfries. In 1857 he became the first Commissioner in Lunacy in Scotland. Browne was clearly at the cutting edge of the treatment of lunacy in Victorian society and it comes as no surprise that Darwin found his son, Dr J. Crichton Browne, director of 'an immense asylum near Wakefield', a powerful ally in his project.

William Browne sowed the seed, which seems to have lain in the ground until about 1838, when Darwin began to make observations on the subject, reading or re-reading Bell's book around 1844. He was 'already inclined to believe in the principle of evolution' and could not accept that man had been created with muscles specially adapted for the expression of his feelings. He thought that the habit of expressing feelings by certain movements must have been gradually acquired, though now they were innate. But how such habits had been acquired 'was perplexing in no small degree.'

On 27 December 1839 the Darwins' first child, William, was born. Darwin began a notebook recording the infant's expressions (published as *A Biographical Sketch of an Infant* in 1877):

> My first child was born on 27 December 1839 and I at once commenced to make notes on the first dawn of the various expressions he exhibited, for I felt convinced, even at this early period, that the most complex and fine shades of expression must all have a gradual and natural origin.

In 1867 he circulated a questionnaire – 'Queries about Expressions' – to a wide range of recipients. These included 'colonialists', missionaries or protectors of aboriginal peoples and the Medical Officers of regiments serving overseas. Other researchers reprinted and recirculated it three further times.

Darwin had intended to have a chapter on human emotions in *The Descent of Man* but had by now accumulated so much material that it was necessary that it should have its own book.

His Introduction starts by dismissing the notion that man and all other animals are independent creations:

> The community of certain expressions...is rendered somewhat more intelligible, if we believe in their descent from a common progenitor.

As regards methodology:

> The study of Expression is difficult, owing to the movements being often extremely slight, and of a fleeting nature.

He might have said that the limitations of photography in his time made it difficult to provide evidence that was not stilted and solemn, due to the lengthy exposures necessary. Today we have long series of 'reality television', where hidden cameras record every moment, waking and sleeping, of individuals chosen for their expressions of the emotions and thrown together in deliberately contrived stressful situations – just not possible in 1872.

An ingenious way of making the best of a bad job was to use actors. Thus, under 'Helplessness, impotence, shrugging the shoulders', Darwin describes the component movements and goes on to say:

> Though I had often intentionally shrugged my shoulders to observe how my arms were placed, I was not at all aware that my eyebrows were raised and mouth opened, until I looked at myself in a glass; and since then I have noticed the same movements in the faces of others. In the accompanying Plate, Mr Rejlander has successfully acted the gesture of shrugging the shoulders.

Dr Crichton Browne of the West Riding Asylum, on the issue of 'the erection of the hair', provided photographs of two women, one of which was copied as an engraving. This was one subject which did prompt

Darwin to quote from Shakespeare, when Brutus says to the ghost of Caesar: 'That mak'st my blood cold, and my hair to stare.' After the murder of Gloucester in *King Henry VI* Cardinal Beaufort exclaims: 'Comb down his hair: look, look, it stands upright.'

Dr Duchenne of the famous Salpêtrière in Paris administered electric shock treatment to the muscles in the face of an old man and photographed the results. (There was a tussle between Darwin and the publisher over the cost of using photographs, which were more expensive to use than the traditional woodcuts. The Folio Society edition of 1990 interestingly reverted to the use of line drawings made from Dr Duchenne's photographs).

FIG 16: Terror (from a photograph by Dr Duchenne) (*The Expression of the Emotions*)

If we needed it, there is no better evidence of the effectiveness of Darwin as a networker than his association with La Salpêtrière. Surely unique in being the only mental hospital with a star *(Intéressent)* in the *Guide Michelin,* it was set up in 1656 by Louis XIV on the site of a gunpowder works. As a General Hospital for the Poor it was intended to clear the streets of beggars and the like, in effect becoming a prison for the mad, the infirm, the orphaned and prostitutes, all subject to the same harsh regime.

The great church of St Louis is in the middle of the hospital façade. It has a central area with eight bays/chapels radiating out from it. In its heyday Mass would be observed in the middle and the inmates would attend in their categories. So the lunatics would not have to mix with the prostitutes, who would be spared the sight of the beggars and so on. All had access to God, but without distraction. There were no windows below about 20 feet up, either.

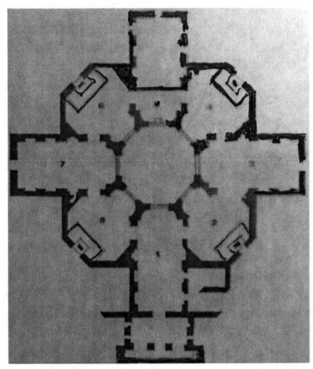

FIG 17: Plan of St Louis' Church, La Salpétrière

In the 18th century the mentally deranged were chained to the walls. In September 1792, revolutionaries from the Faubourg Saint-Marcel set forth with the noble intent of liberating the prostitutes, but liquor got the better of them and instead they dragged out on to the street 45 wretched madwomen and massacred them in an orgy of pointless killing. At the end of the 18th century Philippe Pinel began a reformed treatment for the insane, which won for him and the institution wide acclaim. A century later Professor Charcot (under whom Freud came to study) led a team which furthered the hospital's reputation for research and treatment in advanced neuro-psychiatry. Guillaume Benjamin Amand Duchenne (1806–75) first described the disease we now know as Duchenne muscular dystrophy, the most prevalent of muscular dystrophies, affecting one in 3,500 males. (Females are carriers). 'Intellectual impairment may or may not be present.' No doubt Dr Duchenne found that some of his lunatics were, in fact, suffering from muscle degeneration rather than being insane. His *Mécanisme de la Physionomé Humaine* was an important source book for Darwin.

Armed with such photographs, 'above 20' (24, he writes elsewhere) 'educated persons of various ages and both sexes' were asked by Darwin to identify the emotion associated with each photograph. Intrigued by this, I decided to play the role of Darwin by sending the image to 'educated persons of various ages and both sexes' in my own circle, inviting a one-word response. Of the 20 replies, 12 saw in the picture Horror or Fear, one used Darwin's word – Terror. Other descriptors were: Grief (1), Surprise (2), Shock (1), Fright (1), Amazed Consternation (1), Frustration and Pain (1). Three respondents mentioned *The Scream*. Which brings up another question – where did Munch get his 'inspiration' from? A doctor specialising in the elderly commented:

> amazing what doctors could do in the olden days...Duchenne would be on gardening leave if he did that nowadays!

My little test was no more scientific than Darwin's, nor any less. Has it any value? It would seem to be true that the majority of people today can deduce emotion from appearance. So could Darwin's respondents: '20 registered "intense fright" or "horror"; three said "pain" and one "discomfort." My circle of respondents had a greater range of answers. They used eight terms. This may be a reflection of our greater opportunities to study the emotions through film in its different forms, but none of the additional terms used by today's subjects differs substantially in meaning from Darwin. Altogether, it does look as if this method has something to recommend it.

The nature of evidence is always intriguing. At Lullingstone Roman Villa in Kent was found a roofing tile over which a cat had walked while it was still wet, leaving a clear pawprint. Since it was only a roofing tile it was used and has survived. Although mosaics, a bath, post-holes and the like have been found and preserved no other trace of a living creature, man or beast, has been turned up. The experts cannot tell who lived there, what they believed, what they looked like – but they could, if they wanted, deduce so much from the pawprint of the anonymous cat.

So one speculates about the poor fellow who represented Terror. Who was he? How did he come to be in the Salpêtrière? How did he like the weekly semi-segregated worship in the great church of St Louis? One could conceive of a novel built around him; like Julian Rathbone, whose *Last Great Englishman* begins with the hero giving Darwin some advice about finches before being left behind (by mistake) on the Galapagos. One thing is for sure. The unfortunate subject of FIG 16 did not suffer from Duchenne muscular dystrophy. He was too old. DMD men die young.

Darwin, of course, did not limit his investigation to the picture alone. Referring back to Dr Bell, he has a description of the *platysma myoides* muscle and the effects of its operation. Duchenne called it the 'muscle of fright'. Dr Browne was sceptical. Dr Ogle also, after observing 20 patients in a London hospital just before being put under the influence of chloroform. 'Much perplexed', Darwin 'applied to many obliging correspondents for information.' And so it went on.

Young children were another source of evidence. They showed emotions 'with extraordinary force' and were unspoiled in that older children and adults 'cease to have the pure and simple source from which they spring in infancy.'

As a source of evidence, the insane had similar advantages. They, too, were 'liable to the strongest passions, and give uncontrolled vent to them.' They had another advantage for Darwin's project, they were organised and data collection was easy. Victorian lunatic asylums have a bad press today, we think of them as vast, inhuman barracks where the unfortunate were locked away for the rest of their days. Not all, however, matched this stereotype, there was a move towards enlightenment and Darwin was able to contact several liberal and enlightened asylum directors, notably Dr J. Crichton Browne, son of the William Browne who had criticised Bell the anatomist before the Plinian Society.

Darwin established Browne's credentials, he was in charge of 'an immense asylum near Wakefield and…had already attended to the subject,' making him therefore a powerful ally for Darwin. One of the charms – and perhaps a weakness – of *The Expression of Emotions* is the anecdotal nature of the evidence and Darwin's attributions to individuals. The hand of Crichton Browne can thus be traced throughout the book.

Darwin expected to learn much from study of the great masters of painting and sculpture, since these were close observers of often irrational subjects and had behind them manuals showing how details should be represented. He was, however, disappointed, finding:

> That, in works of art, beauty is the chief object: and strongly contracted facial muscles destroy beauty.

Perhaps he should have travelled more, to Colmar, to the Unterlinden Museum. The first two rooms are harmless enough, with Crucifixions where Christ looks heavenwards with gentle resignation, Madonnas calm and polished hold placid infants and a miscellany of saints suffer horrible deaths with perfect equability. Then we go into the large room which houses the Isenheim altarpiece of Matthias Grünewald. Here Christ hangs in obvious torment, His body distorted by its own weight from hanging for hours on the cross. His mother and Mary Magdalene are ugly with grief at His feet, the latter convulsively twisting her interlaced fingers. On other panels devils displaying strong emotions roast miserable sinners.

Literature might have produced some interesting quotations for Darwin, but he finds little of substance to work on, although he does quote Norfolk, speaking of Cardinal Wolsey, in Shakespeare's *King Henry* VIII:

> My lord, we have stood here observing him:
> Some strange commotion is in his brain:
> He bites his lip and starts;
> Stops on a sudden, looks upon the ground,
> Then lays his finger on his temple; straight
> Springs out into fast gait; then stops again,
> Strikes his breast hard; and soon he casts
> His eye against the moon: in most strange postures
> We have seen him set himself,

progressing from the sublime to the gorblimey by observing: 'A vulgar man often scratches his head when perplexed in mind.' Perhaps using actors to represent emotion was not such a bad idea after all. On the other hand, Shakespeare may have only been describing what actors did in his time, rather than the actual behaviour of an insane person.

To what extent can we accept the expression of emotions at its face value? Remember Hamlet? 'One may smile, and smile, and be a villain.'

Or Richard III? 'For I can smile, and murder while I smile.' Could Darwin have found an actor to illustrate Burns' picture of Tam O'Shanter's wife in the poem of that name?

> ...our hame,
> Where sits our sulky sullen dame,
> Gathering her brows like gathering storm,
> Nursing her wrath to keep it warm?

The questionnaire shows Darwin at his most industrious and persistent. He needed to know whether the same expressions and gestures prevailed among all the races of mankind, especially those with little contact with Europeans. If they did, they were likely to be innate or instinctive. Otherwise, they were likely to have been acquired during early life 'in the same manner as do their languages.' Darwin's 16 questions would hardly pass muster with a contemporary research student, yet they did generate a mass of interesting detail.

Darwin was not content with yes or no answers and frequently wrote back to his correspondents seeking further information or clarification. Gavin de Beer, the editor of his *Autobiography*, says that, when he found anybody who possessed the knowledge that he wanted, he would write letter after letter with question after question, disarmingly interspersed with 'If it would not cause you too much trouble', 'Pray add to your kindness', 'I fear that you will think that you have fallen on a most troublesome petitioner'.

> His correspondents must have felt their hearts sink when the postman brought them a letter with the Downe postmark. Nothing must be allowed to stand in the way of the One Great Subject, and this is why his achievement was so great.

Now for my own little piece of research. Darwin's 16th question was: 'Is the head nodded vertically in affirmation, and shaken laterally in negation?' Darwin's commentary on the results states that these actions 'were innate or instinctive among Anglo-Saxons' and cites as evidence that:

> The blind and deaf Laura Bridgman accompanied her *yes* with the common affirmative nod, and her *no* with our negative shake of the head.

When I worked in Edinburgh we had a constant flow of distinguished visitors who wanted to visit the city and required some official business so that their expenses could be covered. One day I was entertaining two Sri Lankans and was in full flow when I realised that something was wrong. Although I thought I was talking good sense, my visitors appeared to be unhappy with the message I was trying to put across. I stopped and challenged them – 'Are you not happy with what I am saying?' 'No, no, there is no problem. You see, in our country, when we shake our heads, it means we agree, and when we nod it means no.' What would Darwin have made of this? Nature or nurture?

Having amassed his material, Darwin organised it into fourteen chapters, as follows:

I	General Principles of Expression
II	General Principles of Expression continued
III	General Principles of Expression continued
IV	Means of Expression in Animals
V	Special Expressions of Animals
VI	Special Expressions of Man: Suffering and Weeping
VII	Low Spirits, Anxiety, Grief, Dejection, Despair
VIII	Joy, High Spirits, Love, Tender Feelings, Devotion
IX	Reflection, Meditation, Ill-temper, Sulkiness, Determination
X	Hatred and Anger
XI	Disdain, Contempt, Disgust, Guilt, Pride, Helplessness, Patience, Affirmation and Negation
XII	Surprise, Astonishment, Fear, Horror
XIII	Shame, Shyness, Modesty, Blushing
XIV	Concluding Remarks and Summary

To give a flavour of how he deals with a topic I have selected the penultimate chapter, 'Blushing', because, he says: 'Blushing is the most peculiar and the most human of all expressions.' He quickly disposes of the mechanics of blushing:

> ...relaxation of the muscular coats of the small arteries, by which the capillaries become filled with blood. We cannot cause a blush

by any physical means, by any action of the body. It is the mind which must be affected. Blushing is not only involuntary, but the wish to restrain it...actually increases the tendency.

One of the reasons for the popularity of *The Expression of Emotions* is the same as makes reality shows popular; we all have emotions and get vicarious pleasure out of seeing others dealing with them. Blushing gives readers the opportunity for a little mild titillation. Darwin was, of course, completely objective in wanting to learn how far down the body blushes extend, so he enlisted the aid of Sir J. Paget and Dr J. Crichton Browne. The result is a paragraph which must have made many a Victorian bluestocking – in Darwin's words – 'agitated and tremulous.'

After his general introduction Darwin treats us with a wealth of anecdote and supposition under the following headings:

Blushing in the various races of men

Movements and gestures which accompany Blushing

Confusion of mind

The Nature of the Mental States which induce Blushing

Shyness

Moral causes: guilt

Breaches of etiquette

Modesty

Theory of Blushing

Recapitulation

With *The Expression of the Emotions in Men and Animals* Darwin had produced a vast, sprawling opus, full of interesting information, prejudice and idiosyncrasy. A jolly good read but almost impossible to summarise. He did, nevertheless, contrive to slice through the verbiage to arrive at three conclusions or principles about the expression of the emotions. These were:

I   The principle of serviceable associated Habits
     (Movements become so habitual that they are performed, whether or not of any service, whenever the same desire or sensation is felt, even in a very weak degree).

II   The principle of Antithesis
        (The habit of voluntarily performing opposite movements
        under opposite impulses has become fairly established in us
        by the practice of our whole lives).

III   The principle of actions due to the constitution of the Nervous
        System, independently from the first of the Will, and inde-
        pendently to a certain extent of Habit.
        (Direct action of the excited nervous system on the body,
        independently of the will, and independently, in large parts,
        of habit).

It is the fate of the pioneer to see others moving in to claim the territo-ry he opened up under great difficulty. *Expression of the Emotions* was popular enough to warrant a new edition in 1890 but it faded out as new specialists, armed with new methods, entered the field, rejecting or ignoring Darwin's work. Darwin's illustrations – verbal as well as graphic – very quickly began to appear dated.

His reliance on anecdotal data and his means of collecting it were more than suspect. In his three chapters on 'General Principles of Expression' there is a great extended descriptive passage on the behaviour of dogs, illustrated by woodcuts: 'By Mr Riviere'. Suddenly we read: 'Sir W. Scott's famous Scotch greyhound, Maida, had this habit.' This statement leaves Darwin wide open to scholarly criticism on three grounds – the unreliability of the source, the smallness of the sample and factual inac-curacy – Maida was not a greyhound but a Highland staghound.

Darwin did not explain the origin of emotional expressions in terms of their communicative value – no doubt a consequence of his limited study methods.

Darwin was judged guilty of anthropomorphism – the attribution of human behaviour or appearance to an animal, for example, *Winnie the Pooh* – which was taboo for the next generation of anthropologists. Yet as early as 1936 Frank Fraser Darling was saying (in *A Herd of Red Deer*):

The behaviour of one species can show surprising latitude under stress of circumstance, and amongst the higher animals we find response to sets of conditions and a spontaneity of action which we, as so-called rational beings, could not better. In some instances I feel that the most simple explanation of an act of behaviour is to follow the bare outline of our own mental processes in such a situation. I believe the teleological approach to animal behaviour to be dangerous but the current objection to anthropomorphism can be overdone. Who are the people with whom the higher animals are most serene? And who achieve most success in their management and training? Not those who look upon them as automata, but those who treat them as likeable children of our own kind.

Twentieth century relativists questioned that expressions were innate and part of our biology. *The Expression of the Emotions* became part of the nature *v* nurture debate. Margaret Mead, the famous anthropologist, claimed that the same expression signified different emotions in different cultures – as I found with my Sri Lankans. Darwin was accused – at this late stage – of being Lamarckian in suggesting that characteristics acquired in a person's lifetime could be inherited by the progeny.

Darwin's questioning mind produced a work of great interest which is often seen as the foundation stone of ethnography. If not a foundation stone, it has certainly been a quarry, as successive generations have found in it inspiration to further investigation. Some of his insights have stood the test of time, even though some of his evidence has not.

What is most remarkable is the genesis of the project. From the Plinian Society of the 1820s came the central question which niggled for years till Darwin could turn his massive concentration on its resolution. His Edinburgh days had not been wasted!

CHAPTER EIGHT

Charles Darwin and Patrick Geddes

IF ONE DROPPED IN on a luncheon group at the faculty club of a metropolitan university and asked a dozen scholars: 'Who is Patrick Geddes?' there would probably be a dozen answers, and though some of the answers would be hazy, they would all, I think, be different; and one might get the impression that Professor Geddes is a vigorous institution, rather than a man.

Thus said Lewis Mumford, one of the leading planners of the first half of the 20th century and a disciple of Geddes. In 334 words *Who's Who 1930* (see Appendix) summed up Geddes's achievements while the cover of Philip Boardman's *The Worlds of Patrick Geddes* and the memorial plaque placed on the site of the Geddes birthhouse in Ballater on 2 April 2008 both use the same description: 'Patrick Geddes – Biologist, Town Planner, Re-educator, Peace-warrior.'

Patrick Geddes is a major figure in his own right and could easily distract from my main purpose. For those who have to have an answer now to the question: 'Who was Patrick Geddes?' I refer to An Evolution Chronology at the end of this book and the Appendix cited above.

Patrick Geddes is being used as a case study to answer the obvious question: 'How did a young man from a very modest background in a small provincial city, with the sketchiest of qualifications, break into the upper echelons of the scientific society of his time?' To what extent did Darwin influence and promote the young Geddes? Then I shall try to clarify Geddes's role in the dissemination and interpretation of Darwin's ideas.

The main source for Geddes' early years is Geddes himself, supplemented by the correspondence between John McKail Geddes, Patrick's brother who had emigrated to New Zealand, and the family back in Perth. In 1923 Geddes gave a series of lectures in the United States, which Mumford published in 1925 as six *Talks from My/The Outlook*

Tower in *Survey*, a sociology periodical. (The series started as 'My' and became 'The' Outlook Tower.) *The Education of Two Boys* is the talk of most interest to us today and has proved to be the source upon which all writers on Geddes have drawn.

Geddes was 70 when he wrote the essay; he was trying to prove that his 'education of two boys' was the model and, from our own experiences, we know how selective memory can be. He was also geographically far away from the scenes he was describing:

> As I revise this manuscript, our ship is running along the east
> coast of Sicily, between Messina and Catania.

When Geddes was 74 (in 1928) *Young Barbarian,* the Perth Academy school magazine, published *Memories and Reflections,* written at Montpellier. Again, we must be aware of the selectivity of memory dulled by time and space. (We should also be conscious that Darwin was 67 when his *Autobiography* was published and therefore exercise suitable caution with its interpretation.)

The two boys in the title are not Geddes' two sons, as one might suppose. They are Alasdair (the elder son, killed in the First World War) and Geddes himself. He describes his childhood and upbringing on the slopes of Kinnoull Hill where 'the wise and gentle father' walked with him around the garden of Mount Tabor Cottage on the Sabbath. East of the Tay was a developing leafy suburb of Perth, ancient market and county town, major railway and textile centre. Geddes' father was a Quartermaster in the Militia, an officer promoted from the ranks, while all around were the big houses of the *gratin* of Perth.

At least two writers – not Scots – have referred to Geddes as the typical 'lad o' pairts' of Scottish history as wished for. He was not. Never did he walk miles barefoot in the snow to attend the wee school with the children of the ploughmen and the laird. Nor did he carry his daily peat for the schoolroom fire. Nor did he follow the conventional trail to university and starvation in a garret, returning on Meal Monday holidays for a new supply of his staple food.

Mount Tabor Cottage was no palace, but neither was it a but-and-ben. It had six rooms with one or more windows and the Geddes family were well enough off to keep a live-in servant, no miserable ragged tweeny, but a mature lass from the next parish. Certainly, in the years after Patrick had left home to seek his fortune, the family circumstances were quite comfortable.[8]

Geddes described a close-knit family life. There probably was little coming and going between the globetrotters in the cottage and the local bourgeoisie in the big houses. There were few children of Patrick's age to 'chum' him to school, or with whom he could play. School was down the hill and across Smeaton's great bridge in Perth, not very close and there were probably few like-minded youngsters around Mount Tabor. The result must have been that Patrick was often a lonely little boy, spending most of his time with older people, although he did write:

> Games were enjoyed, especially the combative, from inter-scholastic snowfights to football, but cricket seemed slow, and golf intolerably old and grownup.

As for formal schooling, Geddes' reminiscences were favourable and, given his objections to the 'cram-exam' system, remarkably conformist. He 'soon tired of Latin', had a good grounding in English, French, Chemistry and – especially – Maths, where he was very well taught, partly in the outdoors.

On the plus side he was encouraged to develop his talents to the full – his brother, writing from New Zealand when Patrick was aged nine, said:

> I am happy...that you are always keeping up your place as a gentleman and scholar. You will soon be fit to come to a decision what you will want to be. Whether philosopher, gardener, astronomer or militiaman.

A year later his brother wrote again:

> Last month being the time of the Perth examination Pat would be very busy and I hope to hear that he has got several prizes,

and,

> I was very glad to hear that you have got three prizes. You richly deserve them. Would you tell me what they are for... Father will be prouder about them than you are yourself.

Young Patrick 'grew up in a garden'. He spent many hours rambling through the woods on Kinnoull Hill and there were long expeditions to the Highlands. There was learning by doing, planting potatoes, making a box and the like. He collected geological and botanical specimens to be examined and stored in his own laboratory at home. A day's excursion to Edinburgh opened his eyes to the excitement of Scotland's past.

When he left school he had a spell working in the local bank, acquiring an understanding of what money could do, while maintaining an indifference to its acquisition for himself, which lasted all his life. Then came a period of 'home studies'. His father – remarkable for a Victorian parent – built for him a workshop and laboratory, when it seemed that adolescent mischief might develop into something worse. He had lessons on cabinet-making in the mornings, attended the School of Art in the afternoons and was encouraged to read voraciously. What and where did he read?

At that time Perth had at least seven circulating libraries as well as an array of good, serious libraries – a Public Library of 1786, a Mechanics' Library founded 1823, the library of the Literary and Antiquarian Society. The Perth Reading Society was another public library, of 1823. The Andersonian Institution (1847) had a library of several hundred volumes 'mostly of a scientific nature'. And there was an *Encyclopedia Perthensis* (1796–1806) in 23 volumes.

The *Second Supplement to the Catalogue of the Perth Mechanics' Library (1876)* included *The Expression of the Emotions in Man and Animals*. By Charles Darwin. Illustrated. London, 1872. 1 volume, and *The Movements and Habits of Climbing Plants*. By Charles Darwin, MA, Illustrated. London, 1875. 1 volume. While Geddes had moved on by 1875 he was certain to have read *Expression of the Emotions*.

FIG 18 shows the cover of *A Most Unsettling Person: An Introduction to the Ideas and Life of Patrick Geddes,* by Paddy Kitchen, reproduced by kind permission of the publisher, Victor Gollancz, an imprint of the Orion Publishing Group. While I (and they) have been unable to trace the source of the portrait it very much looks as if Geddes has been dabbling in some of the ideas Darwin was concerned with in *Expression of the Emotions*.

Reading was a solitary occupation but the Perthshire Society of Natural Science must have influenced Geddes socially as well as intellectually. The Society's minutes show that, on 5 January 1871, Carl Fleckstein, teacher of Modern Languages at Perth Academy, proposed Geddes's name to the

An Introduction to the
Ideas and Life of Patrick Geddes
A MOST UNSETTLING PERSON
Paddy Kitchen

Double Right. *Normal.*

Reversed. *Double Left.*

FIG 18:

Quadro-portrait of Geddes

(*A Most Unsettling Person:
An Introduction to the Ideas
and Life of Patrick Geddes*)

Society and that he became a regular attender. Later that year he left school and in 1872 he was voted on to the Library Committee. The minutes of the Annual Meeting of 1872 record:

> The following books have been added to the library of the Perthshire Society of Natural Science –
> By purchase – '*Descent of Man*' – Darwin.

The Perthshire Society of Natural Science was no collection of rude mechanicals meeting in a back room, trying to pull themselves up by their own bootstraps by discussing dreary Victorian tomes. The President and moving spirit in the foundation of the Society of Natural Science was Dr Francis Buchanan White, a good enough biologist to have applied (but without success) for the chair of Zoology at Owens College, Manchester, the kernel from which Manchester University grew. A later President was Dr James Geikie, Director of the Geological Survey in Scotland and author of *The Great Ice Age and its Relation to the Antiquity of Man*. When he moved on, it was to succeed his brother in the Murchison Chair of Geology and Mineralogy at the University of Edinburgh.

That the Society had a wide remit was demonstrated in the autumn of 1878 when Darwin, in his role as the one-man biology database, was engaged in an interesting quadrangular issue. Having been sent material by a scientist-explorer, Thomas Vernon Wollaston, Buchanan White published a paper on 'Hemipterous fauna of St Helena' in the Proceedings of the Zoological Society of London. Wollaston (1822–78) was a friend of Darwin with interests in insects and islands. He made five long trips to Madeira. The British Museum purchased his Madeiran *Coleoptera* collection. He made two trips to the Canary Islands, then visited the Cape Verde Islands. The trip to St Helena was his last. Having died at Teignmouth on 4 January 1878, the goings-on between Darwin, Hooker and Buchanan White took place in the knowledge of his recent demise.

Buchanan White's paper (full title – 'Contributions to a Knowledge of the Hemipterous Fauna of St Helena and Speculations on its Origin') comprises 35 pages plus a page of illustrations. In the Descriptive section of 16 pages he makes it clear that Wollaston, a few months before his death, handed over his collection to Buchanan White 'for determination', with directions that a 'set of types' be placed in the British Museum and that the new species be described in a single paper and not piecemeal. This had now been done with this paper. There followed lists and notes, with seven new genera and 24 species named and described, with the authority of Buchanan White. Several have the specific *sanctae-helenae*, there is also a *wollastoniana* and a *wollastoni*. Part 1 is Speculative, and this is where the trouble must have crept in.

In a letter of 23 September 1878 (from the Perthshire Society for Natural Science Collection, reproduced here by kind permission of Perth Museums and Art Gallery), Darwin commented on White's paper, as follows:

Dear Sir,
I have now read your paper, and I hope that you will not think me presumptuous in writing another line to say how excellent it seems to me. I believe that you have largely solved the problem

of the affinities of the inhabitants of this most interesting little island, and this is a delightful triumph.
Dear sir, Yours faithfully,
Ch Darwin

Darwin suggested on 5 October that Hooker should read the paper. The Canary Islands and South Africa were referred to and the outcome seems to have been a rejection by Hooker of White's explanation. That he replied to Darwin on 7 October seems to suggest that he had already read Buchanan White's paper and had made up his mind about it. (The *Beagle* had returned via St Helena. Darwin noted the imbalance between endemic and introduced plants – 52 and 746 respectively – and the massive environmental changes as a result of human intervention).

This little interchange illustrates two points. In late Victorian times a provincial, mainly amateur, society could still play a role in the advancement of knowledge. We also see Darwin the networker in operation. Not only did he pursue his own lines of enquiry, he busied himself constantly with anyone prepared to be interested at home and in other countries.

The regard the Society held for Darwin is shown by an entry of the Minute Book for 4 May 1882:

> Dr Buchanan White moved, seconded by the Secretary, that the Society record the regret it feels at the death of Dr Darwin the greatest Naturalist of the age.

On 3 February 1881, 'Patrick Geddes, FRSE, Assistant to Professor of Botany, Edinburgh', by now a resident of Edinburgh, became a Corresponding Member, no doubt wishing to continue an established attachment having left the city. His proposer was James Geikie, President of the Society. That the link remained is shown by the fact that Geddes met Sir Robert Pullar in Perth in 1900, receiving £100 towards his entry for the *Exposition Universelle* in Paris.[9] In 1883 both Geikie and Geddes returned to Perth for a three-day *Conversazione* on the opening of the Society's Museum to the public. Geikie started the celebration on the Thursday, while Geddes opened the Saturday session with an address on the 'Study of Biology'. Dr Wilson was to have talked on the 'Challenger Expedition' but was unavoidably absent, Geddes stepping into the breach by 'exhibiting the limelight views' of Dr Wilson.

Geddes had undergone an education of 'Head, Heart and Hand'

long before the advent of Dewey. He attended Edinburgh University for a week before rejecting what it had to offer. In rejecting the conventional way forward he demonstrated a remarkable self-confidence. Having been reading Thomas Huxley's 'lay sermons' he formed a 'burning desire' to study under Huxley in London. The next move was to the Royal School of Mines (from 1907 Imperial College of Science), where he had to do a probationary year before becoming, in his second year, 'something of a real assistant' to Huxley.

Having seen Patrick Geddes, the young man from the very modest background in provincial Perth, with the sketchiest of qualifications, into the Royal School of Mines, it seems appropriate to ask – is that all? Was there perhaps another influence which helped to smooth the way for the young Geddes. Was there a hidden hand at work?

Picture the first day at the Royal School of Mines with a room full of bright young sparks, many from affluent backgrounds, products of the public schools or with the sophistication of having spent all their lives in the capital. Into this group comes this shabby provincial with an impenetrable accent, yet who has something about him which takes him through the ruck to the position of Huxley's protégé. Probably all were clever, all were hard-working, could it be that Geddes had an aura about him that emanated, not only from his liberal education and the loving support of his family, but from his consciousness that his father and family were specially favoured from an association with the Queen and Prince Albert?

Where was Patrick Geddes born? The Lasat Word? (Walter Stephen, Hills of Home, Edinburgh, 2008) suggests that Geddes had such an aura and gives the evidence for it in meticulous detail. It is a complex tale involving the discharge of Alexander Geddes on medical grounds, his being head-hunted for the post of supervisor of the works rebuilding Balmoral, deliberate falsification of Army records and subsequent corrections in another hand, a mysterious increase in pension of 6d a week, a commission into the Royal Perthshire Rifles (Perthshire Militia) three days after its formation, and an Annuity for Meritorious Service of £15 per annum.

At the Royal School of Mines, Geddes was soon put on to his own research. He discovered an error in Huxley's work. Generously, Huxley insisted that Geddes write a paper, with three plates, which Huxley presented to the Zoological Society as a correction of his work by a pupil.

Huxley found a place for Geddes as a demonstrator at Kew and put him up for the Sharpe Scholarship at University College. Here took place the first recorded meeting of Darwin and Geddes.

To this point there has been much of Huxley but scarcely a mention of Darwin. This is not surprising, given the relationship between Geddes and the two senior figures of contemporary biology. In 1872 the students of Aberdeen University proposed *Mr* Charles Darwin, *Professor* Huxley and eight others for election as Lord Rector. Darwin declined to participate on the grounds of ill health and T.H. Huxley was elected Lord Rector on 14 December 1872. For Geddes, Darwin was familiar through his writings. Otherwise he would have seemed a free spirit, with private means and with little involvement at a high level in important – but time-consuming – organisations (the exception being the Secretaryship of the Geological Society). Huxley was however, in modern management speak, for two years Geddes's superordinate officer, as well as teacher, with whom he was in almost daily contact, who recognised his talent and pushed him forward in his career. Fortunately, Darwin and Huxley were close and in frequent communication and Geddes benefited from their association.

A crucial incident took place in J. Burdon Sanderson's laboratory at University College and was described by Geddes in 1931 (in *Life: Outlines of Biology*) as a 'vivid and memorable lesson in biology.' Geddes was filling in some spare moments by examining samples of pond-water through a microscope. The first slide revealed nothing much of interest and he was about to get a fresh sample when someone gently pushed him aside. A big beard came over his shoulder, and there was Darwin! The famous scientist, who had come in unnoticed, looked in the barren microscope field without saying a word. Then he broke out:

> ...positively shouting for joy: 'I say! They're moving, they're moving! Sanderson! Sanderson! Come and see, they're MOVING! Look at that!'
> Was not here a vivid and memorable lesson in biology – this literally Pan-ic intoxication of ecstasy, in our oldest of veterans, greatest of masters, before this simplest spectacle of life?

Early in 1878 Geddes had 'a sharp illness' and was advised to take a holiday out of London. Huxley sent him to Roscoff and its marine laboratory station, to which he returned for a summer's work. Then came the Sorbonne and a week in Naples, studying their marine laboratory, towards which, in 1873, Darwin had contributed £75. On an invitation from Professor Cossar Ewart of Aberdeen Geddes now established the Scottish Zoological Station at Cowie, south of Aberdeen, the first in Great Britain. Geddes' oldest brother was a banker in Mexico City and Geddes was now awarded £50 by the British Association to conduct palaeontological and zoological research in Mexico. He collected crayfish for Huxley, assorted reptiles and crustaceans for the British Museum and specimens of flora for himself.

In Mexico overwork and cumulative eye strain, exacerbated by the excessively bright sunlight, brought about a collapse in Geddes' health. For a time he was a blind invalid. Although he recovered it was clear that he was no longer capable of putting in long hours at the microscope.

Returning to Edinburgh he had a succession of posts, more teaching than researching, in botany, zoology and natural history. He wrote voluminously and engaged in a variety of enterprises which might have been seen as career distractors. In 1879 he had applied (unsuccessfully) for the newly created Chair of Zoology at Queen's College, Manchester. He now cast around frantically for similar posts which would reflect his growing competence and experience. This is where we can now perceive the relationship with Darwin.

In 1880 Geddes wrote to Darwin asking permission to copy figures for an article on 'Insectivorous Plants' in *Encyclopaedia Britannica*. Having been sent a reprint of the article, Darwin, on 9 December 1881, wrote as follows (in Letter 13542 of the Darwin Correspondence Project):

> Dear Sir,
> You were so kind as to send me a few days ago your article in the *Encyclopaedia Britannica*. I have now looked through it and it seems to me wonderfully well done, and you have managed to give in the space a surprising amount of information.
>
> Permit me to add that I read with admiration your researches on the presence of chlorophyll in the animal kingdom.
>
> I remain, dear Sir, Yours faithfully,
> Charles Darwin.

James Geikie commented to Geddes on this exchange:

I hear with very great pleasure what you say as to old Father Darwin. His letters are very precious...

In 1882 Geddes applied for the Chair of Natural History in Edinburgh. Three weeks before he died, Darwin supported the application (in Letter 13746 of the Darwin Correspondence Project) thus:

Down, 27 March 1882

Dear Sir,

I have read several of your biological papers with very great interest, and I have formed, if you will permit me to say so, a high opinion of your abilities. I can entertain no doubt that you will continue to do excellent service in advancing our knowledge in several branches of science. Therefore I believe that you are well fitted to occupy any chair of natural history, for I am convinced that example is fully as important as precept for students.

I remain, dear Sir, Yours faithfully,
Charles Darwin

Late in 1887 the Regius Chair of Botany at Edinburgh fell vacant. For Geddes this was the ideal chair in the ideal place and, for the fifth time, at least, he prepared his formal application. 'The Letter of 1888' is an impressive printed document of 100 pages. Thirty-five leading scientists from Great Britain and the continent wrote in support of Geddes. Darwin's letter of 1882 was re-used, as was Huxley's, which included the following paragraph:

Mr Patrick Geddes was at one time a distinguished student of my class. I have a very high opinion of his abilities; and I am well aware that his knowledge is unusually varied and extensive.

Testimonials rolled in, solicited and unsolicited, from seven educationists, 10 physicians, physiologists and pathologists, five well-known former pupils, 23 university extension students at Dunfermline. A collective letter was signed by 56 colleagues. The bibliography listed three books and 42 papers, but what is very significant is that distracting titles on statistics, economics, capital and labour, cooperation v socialism and John Ruskin were excluded.

What happened to the monumental application of Geddes is uncertain; what is certain is that Isaac Bayley Balfour was appointed to the Edinburgh chair and J. Martin White, a boyhood friend of Geddes, endowed him with the Martin White Chair of Botany at University College, Dundee. Geddes was paid half the salary of a full-time professor, but taught for only part of the year while an assistant was paid to handle the rest. As Boardman says:

> Geddes could earn his academic cake in Dundee, so to speak, and
> eat it for three-quarters of the year anywhere else he wished.

Geddes could now enter a long period with a measure of status and modest security, but with the freedom to range around at home and abroad exploring the interests wider than biology that were now engrossing him.

This is the point where we should stop and examine the factors which had brought Geddes to 'the top of the greasy pole' at the age of 34.

How influential had Darwin been in helping Geddes to this significant position? Birth and upbringing were important; a secure, serious home with supportive parents, an older sister who devoted her time to supporting her talented younger brother, two enterprising older brothers who went out to seek their fortunes in Mexico and New Zealand – successfully. He had a good basic education which was enriched by the informal activities encouraged by 'the wise father' and the period of 'home studies'. In Perth was a network seriously interested in science and through this Geddes was able to meet Darwin through reading his books and discussing his ideas with fellow-enthusiasts, some of very high calibre.

In London, fortified with the special self-confidence that comes with proximity to the great ones of this world, he first satisfied and then became a protégé of Huxley. The scene in Sanderson's laboratory started the second phase of the Geddes/Darwin relationship. There was the Grand Old Man of British science looking down Geddes' microscope and whooping away like a child! If at no other time, Geddes must have learned the importance of enthusiasm and admired the humility of a man great enough to unbend before others in the search for knowledge and understanding.

Now Geddes had a loose association with Darwin. Huxley made

available the first formal steps in Geddes's career, but Geddes kept in touch with Darwin and it must have been known in the appropriate circles that here was a young man worth watching. The 'referee's report' (Letter 13746), although it was only one of several and did not produce the desired result, is quite a remarkable document. Despite the formality of the language of the period, it shows that Darwin really knew and approved of Geddes' work and thought that the best was yet to come. Darwin did not scatter references around like confetti. He declined to support Dr Buchanan White's application to Owens College, on the grounds that he had no personal acquaintance with him. According to Melvyn Bragg's programme on BBC Radio 4, when Dr Grant, of his Edinburgh days, now Professor Grant, applied for a post Darwin refused to recommend him because of his homosexuality.

Critics of Geddes might say that Darwin knew Geddes too well – by alluding to 'several branches of science' he might have been sounding a warning bell about his spreading his talents too thinly. Again, in juxtaposing 'example' and 'precept' was he anticipating the McLuhan 'Medium and message' debate? Or was he merely harping back to his own days at Edinburgh?

The letter is dated 27 March 1882 and Darwin died on 19 April. It must have been one of the last pieces of business he transacted before he died. Yet it is as carefully considered and clearly expressed as anything else he wrote. This surely typified:

the simple, childlike, painstaking, effective Charles Darwin, who established himself presently at the head of living English naturalists.

CHAPTER NINE

Patrick Geddes and Charles Darwin

I HAVE TAKEN A very simplistic line in trying to assess Geddes' success in repaying his debt to Darwin by interpreting for the next generation his contribution to knowledge about and understanding of evolution. I have simply scoured around for Geddes' written comments. But Geddes, although a prolific writer, is not an easy read and a full understanding could only be achieved through careful study of Geddes' actions and activities. Like most of us, attitudes and ideas of others become absorbed into our own intelligence until we cannot say where any thought originated. Darwin was by no means the only influence on Geddes.

From Darwin himself Geddes formulated the Planning Model (the ever evolving study of reality tested periodically against public participation) for which he is hailed as 'Father of Planning'. From the generation after Darwin, Häckel of Jena offered the concept of the interaction between the organism and the environment, while Bergson of Paris identified the *élan vital* or creative impulse. From this Geddes identified the importance of intuition and impulsive action as a trigger for evolutionary mutation in sociological terms.

Auguste Comte (1798–1857) was another Huxley protégé who argued that all sciences passed through a theological, then a metaphysical and then a positive or experiential stage. From him Geddes acquired an approach to the study of cities based on empirical research and inductive reasoning, aimed towards social improvement. In my simple way I see this as Geddes' symbolic three doves and his triad of Sympathy, Synthesis and Synergy – Synergy being putting the plan into action by all working together. The anarchists, Kropotkin and Réclus, purveyed mutual aid and cooperation. They convinced Geddes that regeneration in depressed areas comes, not from competition, but from mutual aid and collaboration. Communities must be empowered, rather than wait for government or charitable agencies.

Réclus was a refugee from the Paris Commune, a presence in Geddes' Outlook Tower and a geographer of international importance – he was a prime mover in the establishment of modern weather forecasting through an undersea telegraph from the Azores. Through Réclus, Geddes was involved in Bakunin's confraternity for anti-authoritarian socialism, theosophists and the founder of the Ba'hai faith. Geddes tutored Annie Besant in biology in the evenings when he was at the Royal School of Mines. In India, she was involved in the Indian independence movement and drew Geddes into contact with Gandhi, who accepted Geddes' regional approach but did not share his enthusiasm for planting trees.

Most importantly, Geddes' ideas were embedded in a complex of practical projects – the Outlook Tower (at once college, museum and laboratory), summer meetings, exhibitions, conservative surgery, greening the environment, city plans in several countries, his Scots College in Montpellier, even masques and pageants.

Geddes' comments on Darwin and evolution are set out in a roughly chronological order and this gives us the opportunity to discern an evolution of views on evolution. Geddes started by being inspired by Darwin and his works but, as we shall see, he moved on to reject some of the outcomes of Darwinism. His initial statements accurately report on the content of Darwin's work and the views of his critics. He moves on to consider greater refinement and qualification of the original ideas, notably introducing more subjective factors to the operation of natural selection. These positive notions hold sway till, in 1915, there is a lament for the way in which Darwinism had been interpreted – Geddes would have said abused – by the Great Powers.

In the 1880s Patrick Geddes was thrashing around in all directions, trying to establish himself satisfactorily in the academic world, initiating various educational and sociological schemes, getting married and starting a family. He did a great deal of writing, partly because he was an educator and communicator, and partly because it was paid. ('Hack work was obligatory for men of science without Darwin's deep pocket.')

One of the spin-offs for Edinburgh from the Enlightenment was the establishment of a serious publishing industry. The first edition of the *Encyclopaedia Britannica* was completed in 1771 and expanded through various editions and owners until the ninth ('Scholar's') edition of 1875–89, the last to be produced in Scotland, with 1,100 contributors.

William and Robert Chambers began *Chambers Encyclopaedia* in 1859. Aimed at a more popular market, it appeared in 520 weekly parts at 1 1/2d each and had over 100 distinguished contributors.

In April 1880 *Encyclopaedia Britannica* commissioned an article from Geddes on 'Insectivorous Plants' and over the next few years he contributed more articles to the *Britannica* and to *Chambers Encyclopaedia* –11 and 22 respectively. Geddes would therefore have gained authority by his having been asked to write for these prestigious publications. His contributions would have gained the authority of having been part of these great repositories of knowledge. (The third kind of authority – charismatic authority – was conveyed in every action he performed.) His articles had a wide currency at a certain level of society for a considerable time – the 1923 edition of *Chambers Encyclopaedia* was the last to contain Geddes material.

Let us start with 'Darwin' from *Chambers' Encyclopaedia*. 'An English naturalist of the highest eminence' is the first statement and almost the last is: 'Darwin's knowledge was no less remarkable than his caution in statements.' Between come his background, his education, the *Beagle* interlude, his research and publications, his honours and achievements:

> In 1859, Darwin's name became 'familiar as a household word'
> to the mass of educated and semi-educated Englishmen,

with the publication of *The Origin of Species,* which Geddes summarises in one monster sentence. Controversy, partial acceptance and consequent changes are described in three lines. We are reminded that the full title of Darwin's great book is *The Origin of Species by Means of Natural Selection, or the Preservation of Favoured Races in the Struggle for Life,* falling into three sections; the bland, the controversial and, for its time, the outrageous.

'Darwinian Theory' is a presentation of facts in a clear prose style, which Geddes sadly lost as he fell deeper and deeper into sociology. He gives a valid account of the history of this theory and an excellent summary of the arguments and the evidence within the *Origin of Species*. His summary of how Darwin's views were received by followers and opponents is equally balanced.

He quoted Huxley – that not a single fact had been found that was 'irreconcilable with Darwinian theory' – but had to point out that this 'universal acceptance is not without its universally distributed exceptions.' He included Darwin's assertion that:

> The theory of evolution by natural selection is no more inimical to religion than is that of gravitation,

and quotes Darwin's *Envoy;*

> There is a grandeur in this view of life, with its several powers, having been originally breathed by the Creator into a few forms, or into one; and that... from so simple a beginning endless forms most beautiful and most wonderful have been, and are being, evolved.

'Evolution' is a substantial (7-page) summing up of answers from theology, philosophy, psychology, the social sciences and modern science and concepts from astronomy, chemistry, geology and, above all, biology. Geddes gives a synopsis of Darwinism, warning of confusion between Evolution and Darwinism, and takes issue with Huxley and his well-known assertion that:

> From the point of view of the naturalist the world is on about the same level as a gladiator's show.

There is a piquancy in his reference (in *Chambers Encyclopaedia*) to Robert Chambers:

> Wells in 1813 and Patrick Matthew in 1831 forestalled Darwin in suggesting the importance of natural selection, but their buried doctrines were of much less practical importance than those of Robert Chambers, the long unknown author of the *Vestiges of Creation* (1844–53). His hypothesis of evolution emphasised the growing or evolving powers of the organisms themselves, which developed in rhythmic impulses through ascending grades of organisation, modified at the same time by external circumstances acting with most effect on the generative system.

Let us stay for a moment with Huxley and Geddes' debt to him and, by implication, to Darwin. Geddes' chosen master provided a superb training and pushed him along a career path. Huxley, according to William Irvine in *Apes, Angels and Victorians*:

could think, draw, speak, write, inspire, lead, negotiate and wage multifarious war against earth and heaven with the cool professional ease of an acrobat supporting nine people on his shoulders at once.

But Geddes had doubts that he was too much of a necrologist, too limited by skeletons. Never were his students sent outside the laboratory to study living things, even though Kensington Gardens were just outside. Huxley was no self-deceiver and on one occasion, after a particularly brilliant demonstration, was said to have mumbled, half to himself: 'You see, I should have been an engineer.'

Geddes had doubts about 'survival of the fittest' – the philosopher Herbert Spencer's coinage replacing 'natural selection' – and the poetic 'Nature red in tooth and claw' from Tennyson's *In Memoriam*. *The Evolution of Sex* suggests that, as well as struggle, cruelty and selfishness in evolution, there is also cooperation; and 'that 'creation's final law' is not struggle but love.'

S.A. Robertson, a former student at Geddes' *Collége des Ecossais*, paid 'A Scottish Tribute' on the death of Geddes in 1932:

> Even a noble soul like Huxley could see in life essentially a 'gladiator's show.' Geddes...challenged the verdict in his books, in his lectures, in the flood of vivacious speech which leaped from him like a fountain. I recall the thrill which went through an audience as he traced the basal feature of all life to be the sacrifice of the mother for her offspring and closed by saying...'So life is not really a gladiator's show; it is rather – a vast mothers' meeting!'

In the Chambers 'Evolution' entry examples were produced suggesting that 'evolution is primarily a materialised ethical process'. With moral optimism Geddes concluded that:

> ...it is possible to interpret the ideals of ethical progress – through love and sociality, co-operation and sacrifice, not as mere utopias contradicted by experience, but as the highest expressions of the central evolutionary process of the natural world.

For the *Encyclopaedia Britannica* Geddes provided an eight-page article on 'Variation and Selection' – 'Evolution' having already been written up by another. Geddes' concern was with the determinant factors of evolution and the mechanism of the evolutionary process. The time had been ripe for *The Origin of Species*. *Vestiges of Creation* had gone through 10 editions in 10 years and the first edition of *The Origin of Species* was taken up on the first day. Geddes analyses *The Origin of Species* and the theory of Natural Selection and Variation under domestication and in nature. The struggle for existence is described and the survival of the fittest, he says, 'is unquestionably a *vera causa.*' Here Geddes is using 'true cause', or 'sacred cause' as Desmond and Moore entitle their book *Race, Slavery and the Quest for Human Origins,* in a special sense.

Thus his conclusion is that the survival of the fittest is an important concept worth pursuing, but in typically Geddesian fashion he muddies the waters by immediately using 'cause' in a different sense. In the same article he denies that the existence of competition in nature and organic progress are cause and effect.

Wallace and, particularly, Huxley are examined in some detail before Geddes covers Darwin's views on variation and notes how ideas on variation and natural selection were moving on rapidly although 'natural selection seems more than ever to be our only possible clue.'

Geddes, like Darwin, was unaware of the work of Mendel (see note 7). Therefore, Darwin's views and his own read as being woolly, idiosyncratic and anecdotal. Thus he qualifies Darwin's 'indefinite variation' without coming up with a positive alternative.

After lengthy coverage of the Laws of Variation Geddes concludes by repeating that competition in nature and organic progress are not necessarily cause and effect and suggests that environmental and social factors also play their part.

> The ideal of Evolution is thus an Eden; and, although competition can never be wholly eliminated, and progress must thus be asymptotic, it is much for our pure natural history to see no longer struggle, but love, as creation's final law.
>
> While ceasing to speak of indefinite variation we may of course still conveniently retain the rest of the established phraseology and continue to speak of 'natural selection' and of 'survival of the fittest,' always provided that...we make the transition from the self-regarding to the other-regarding.[10]

Other comments on Darwin crop up in some odd contexts. In *The Evolution of Sex* (1889, co-authored with J. Arthur Thomson (1860–1931)) Geddes has moved on, perhaps influenced by Thomson. The Darwinian conception of indefinite variation brought about through the haphazard working of natural selection, resulting in an unlimited number of forms of life, is replaced by the restated theory of organic evolution. Certain definite laws of growth limit variation to definite forms, so that evolution becomes an orderly, and even predictable, process. The two main forces are nutrition and reproduction: the desire to preserve self and the desire to perpetuate the species.

Geddes' moral optimism could be trying. *Every Man His Own Art Critic,* written for the Manchester and Glasgow Exhibitions of 1887 and 1888, shows Geddes at his most eclectic and irritating. In 58 pages he rampages round the science of colours, the art of seeing, criticism of individual paintings in the Exhibition, applying generous doses of biology and philosophy. Of a symbolic picture of *Pan and Psyche* Geddes lyrically recalls that:

> although great Pan is dead his avatar (Darwin) was but lately with us to link anew the life of man and beast and grass. Shall we listen, as he did, to the complex piping of the old woodland Pan with an ear which strives to know its many notes and changeful melodies? Or shall our souls ever be lifted from the hurrying stream of vicissitude into the presence of the All?

Chapters in Modern Botany (1893) – Geddes's only textbook – has a throwaway remark about Darwin as a teacher. 'Were it worthy,' he says of his little book, 'it should be dedicated to the memory of Darwin', and laments how hard it is to organise a morphological training that is 'truly Darwinian in spirit from the beginning.'

During the First World War Geddes used his Summer Meetings to organise his thoughts on 'Wardom' and 'Peacedom', published as a 20-page article in the *Sociological Review.* He saw the war as the logical outcome of 19th century Darwinism. British and German minds were dazzled by the 'impressive nature-myth' of tooth-and-claw competition which Darwin and his followers mainly saw in organic evolution. The whole trend of natural science and politics for half a century was based on half-truths and guided by colossal errors of interpretation. Darwin had read nature largely in terms of industrial conflict, of economic survival of the fittest and in turn, the industrialists and economists found in Darwin's projection of their system upon nature the justification for continuing in their ways. German scientists and Prussian imperialists then went all out in adapting this British-industrial conception of evolution to their *Kultur* and their goal of world-dominion. And since 1914 the Prussian statecraft of brute force had openly been hurling this Darwinism of 'might is right' back at the Allies.[11]

A last collaboration with J. Arthur Thomson resulted in *Life: Outlines of General Biology* (1931), a major farewell (combined ages – 147 years) in which Darwin is praised as a lover and understander of nature. Geddes relates a favourite, and illuminating, anecdote.

Having invited some young scientists to his country home Darwin spent a whole evening 'questioning each and drawing him out on his subject; for no man was more open and eager to learn.' Then, leaning back on his chair, Darwin said:

> 'I am always feeling my ignorance, but never have I had it more strongly brought home to me than tonight. You have surprised me! – and again and again! What you, (pointing in turn to each) know about cryptograms, and you tell me about phanerogams, and you about bacteriology, and you about embryology, and you about fishes, and so on, is most interesting! It's something astonishing! You do indeed make me feel my ignorance, and what I have missed!'
>
> Pause: then jumping up from his chair, and with thump on table: 'But – damn you! – there's not a Naturalist in the whole lot of you!'

Darwin's influence on Geddes clearly operated at three levels. Like thousands of others Geddes read Darwin and discussed his reading in a like-minded network. They had a loose professional relationship, in which Geddes was the eager young beaver and Darwin the benign sage. But the greatest influence, as spelt out by Geddes in some of the incidents already described at some length, was the demonstration of excitement and enthusiasm in the face of the natural world.

How successful was Geddes in repaying the debt by interpreting for the next generation Darwin's contribution to knowledge and understanding?

Perhaps another eager young beaver could devise an index and work it out. I cannot. One could find out how many copies of the encyclopaedias were sold, but how many read Geddes' contributions? And of these, how many understood them? Geddes never wrote a bestseller. His books did well enough but were destined for a narrow readership. But, again, how many would have had time for the *Sociological Review* early in 1915 when the Great Powers were slugging it out all across Europe and young men were queueing up to get into uniform?

Morningside Cemetery in Edinburgh is the resting place of many Victorians who sallied forth to set the world to rights and who came back to die in the land of their birth. On the tombstone of one of Florence Nightingale's followers is an epitaph which, suitably adapted, would sum up Geddes' role in promulgating Darwin's thinking:

He did what he could.

Conclusion

ON THE LAST PAGE of the best-known book about an Edinburgh mentor, *The Prime of Miss Jean Brodie*, by Muriel Spark, we find an enquiring young man interviewing Sister Helena of the Transfiguration through the grille in her convent. He asks:

> 'What were the main influences of your school days, Sister Helena? Were they literary or political or personal? Was it Calvinism?'

Sandy said: 'There was a Miss Jean Brodie in her prime.'

Miss Jean Brodie was a good teacher who set high standards. Miss Jean Brodie was a frustrated spinster who fantasized before her pupils. Miss Jean Brodie opened their eyes to a world of beautiful things. Miss Jean Brodie forced her views on to formative minds and humiliated the weaker vessels in the class. Miss Jean Brodie was a thorn in the flesh of her conventional head teacher. How should she have been rated as a mentor?

By the same token, we have dipped into the life of Charles Darwin and come across an array of individuals who had, or should have had, an influence in the training of the young scientist and the subsequent sharpening up or dissemination of his ideas. Was there a big idea uniting the succession of contacts between him and his mentors, or was his development a succession of chance encounters, some positive, some negative and others best forgotten?

Edinburgh University would be the first place to look for mentors. Following his brother Erasmus, young Charles was sent there to study and – if we are to believe his testimony given in old age – did not enjoy the experience. Yet here we encounter the first of several ambiguities in Darwin's relationships. He was so critical of his formal course that he was allowed to drop out after two sessions. Professor Jameson was a particular target, but mainly on the grounds of his methods. (Although Darwin did react against his unfortunate rejection of Hutton's *Theory of the Earth* and its findings.) Darwin's contemporaries were more than content to be driven hard by such mentors of great authority and energy, leaders in their fields, and there is every evidence to suggest that Darwin may not have enjoyed his course, but he certainly benefited from it.

Darwin was more conscious of the value of the informal curriculum. The Plinian Society gave him the opportunity to spread his wings and seeds were sown there that were to develop many years later. Dr Grant was a companion and leader in field studies, yet, many years later, Darwin was mealy-mouthed about him in the *Autobiography* and declined to report in his favour. The 'blackamoor' who conducted the taxidermy classes successfully taught the skills necessary in the 19th century for a practical naturalist. Perhaps more importantly, Darwin learnt from him that a black man could co-exist in a white society if he had the status of an expert or a craftsman.

At Cambridge Darwin was the gentleman amateur, half-heartedly moving towards a church living where he could be a naturalist like Gilbert White of Selborne. From Buckland he learnt of the excitement and variety of the animal kingdom. Sedgwick took him up, gave him geological experience in the field and pushed towards HMS *Beagle*. Unfortunately, the nature of Cambridge at that time, and of the eminent divines – Buckland, Sedgwick and Henslow – was inimical to lateral thinking about creation and evolution. An already cautious tendency was reinforced by the need for circumspection. Darwin was forced to live a kind of intellectual double life in which he appeared to conform on the surface while trying to develop his own ideas by subterfuge.

On the *Beagle* there was Fitzroy, an intellectually stimulating companion, although the length of the voyage was only one factor in the decline of the relationship. Also on the *Beagle* was Lyell's *Principles of Geology,* from which grew a relationship in which, first one, then the other, was the mentor. And yet, when Lyell died, Darwin's overt reaction was lukewarm and partial.

Chambers was never a formal mentor of Darwin, but Darwin certainly learned from him. When *Vestiges of Creation* appeared, Darwin was miffed because he already had 200 pages of his evolution written, his thunder had been stolen and he would have to start again. One of the things he had learned was the need for scholarly respectability and he set off to research and publish the last word on barnacles.

Darwin publicly rejected *Vestiges*, but was careful to dissect the book in private so that he could avoid Chambers' mistakes in fact and in presentation. One of their interchanges would bear closer examination.

Darwin had published and read a paper on Glen Roy. Although it was unsound he still stuck to his guns and, when he heard that Chambers was openly interested in Glen Roy, called on Chambers and gave him advice. Immediately he got home he received by post an anonymous copy of the anonymous *Vestiges*. Darwin must have deduced who the donor was, and therefore the identity of the author. When *Ancient Sea Margins* was published Darwin wrote to Chambers congratulating him. Yet, the day after the Advancement of Science meeting at Oxford where Chambers had been flattened by the Cambridge divines, Darwin weighed in to criticise *Vestiges* and its still (officially) anonymous author.

Earlier the question was asked whether there was a big idea in the influences on Darwin's development, or whether it reflected a series of chance meeting and happenings. From the above it would seem that there are two such ideas, one big, the other common.

Many of Darwin's mentors were children or grandchildren of the Scottish Enlightenment. They would have agreed on the fundamental importance of human reason and combined it with a rejection of any authority which could not be justified by reason. They would have held to a belief in the ability of man to affect changes for the better in society and nature, guided always by reason. Consciously or unconsciously, from Hutton onwards, these notions were passed on to Darwin – although their eventual acceptance caused him much agony, of both body and soul. Compare the Cambridge divines.

At a regrettably human level, few teachers expect visits from successful former pupils, telling them how grateful they are for all that has been done for them. Successful people like to think they made their own success and Darwin's grudging comments on some of his mentors reflect this attitude.

End Notes

1   Down House in the village of Down, in Kent, was Darwin's home. To avoid confusion with three other English Downs, the Post Office address was changed to Downe, although Darwin continued to use Down as the house name. The magnitude of Darwin's correspondence must have been a sore trial for the Down, or Downe, postman.

2   Lytton Strachey (1880–1932) was one of the Bloomsbury Group of writers. In *Eminent Victorians* (1918) he started the trend in debunking everything Victorian which lasted until the demolition of the Euston Arch in 1961 and the poetry of John Betjeman reminded the British public of what had been thrown away.

3   George Combe was reputed to be no 3 in the team. This was denied by Chambers and Nichol in 1859, by which date Combe had died.

4   Caspar David Friedrich (1774–1840) was one of the founders of German Romantic art. Typically his pictures convey a great stillness in which tiny human figures, or a lone watcher, are confronted by great forests almost concealing a slender crucifix or church, by a winter landscape with a twisted pine or a prehistoric tomb, by calm seas reflecting the moon, or by chalk cliffs overlooking the Baltic.

       Friedrich and Weber were both in Dresden in the 1820s and Friedrich's posters for the Berlin premiere of *Der Freischütz* (see note 5) are still the basis for modern stage sets.

5   Carl Maria von Weber (1786–1826) – a Romantic name for a Romantic composer. The son of a consumptive mother, a congenital hip disease gave him a limp for life – like Byron, the supreme Romantic. One of the most progressive composers of the early 19th century and a great virtuoso pianist, Weber founded the German operatic tradition, clearing the way for Wagner.

       He died a suitably Romantic death of consumption (tuberculosis) and self-sacrifice in London in his 40th year. He knew he was very gravely ill and that travel would almost certainly finish him off, but he had a wife and family and there was money to be made in the British capital. To the critic Böttiger he said – 'It's all one! Whether I go or not, in a year I'm a dead man. But if I go, my children will eat when their father's dead, and if I stay they'll starve. What would you do in my place?' On 16 February he left Dresden and fewer than four months later he was dead. But in that time his opera *Oberon* had been premiered and given a string of performances. There was a series of concerts and personal appearances and he even had the generosity to give a free concert for charity.

6   Gully would make a good subject for a factional novel in the modern style.

James Manby Gully was born in Kingston, Jamaica, the son of a wealthy coffee planter. He was taken to England at six and went to school in Liverpool, then Paris. He studied medicine at Edinburgh from 1825 to 1828. Did he meet Darwin? The classes were huge, but if Gully were coffee-coloured he would certainly have been noticed. Gully went on to the Ecole de Médecine in Paris, then graduated MD at Edinburgh in 1829. As well as running his Water Cure Establishment, Gully was interested in women's suffrage, temperance, mesmerism and spiritualism.

In 1872 he met a young woman named Florence Ricardo (later Florence Bravo). They became secret lovers. After travelling with Gully to Germany, Ricardo became pregnant. Gully performed an abortion, after which their relationship became purely platonic. Florence met, fell in love with and married (in 1875) Charles Bravo. On 18 April 1876 Bravo died of poisoning. The culprit was never discovered. Both Gully and Florence were suspects.

Darwin missed the more sensational side of Gully's career, from 1859 having transferred his allegiance to the new and splendid Ilkley Wells House in Wharfedale where, for example, he sat out the publication of *Origin of Species*. As well as being pulled by the big, new, custom-built facility he probably felt pushed by his unease about the relationship between Gully and his female patients.

A substantial contribution to the Darwin anniversaries is *Darwin in Ilkley* by Mike Dixon and Gregory Radick (The History Press), in which is described Darwin's nine-week stay at Ilkley before and just after the publication of *Origin of Species*.

7   Gregor Mendel (1822–84) – 'father of modern genetics' – studied variation in plants in his monastery garden, resulting in 'Mendel's Laws of Inheritance'. His definitive paper of 1866 was published locally, in Brno, and made little impact. (Only three citations in the next 35 years.)

Mendel was rediscovered about 1900 and rapidly became the accepted explanation of heredity. From about 1930 the 'modern synthesis of evolutionary biology' combined Mendelian genetics with Darwin's theory of natural selection, in much the same way as the concept of 'deep time' had provided the engine for the process of evolution.

After Darwin's death a copy of Mendel's paper, uncut, was found in his library. Darwin published *The Movements and Habits of Climbing Plants* in 1865. Mendel's first experiments were with pea plants. What if Darwin had read Mendel's paper when it arrived? Where might it have led him?

As to 'the selfish gene', *The Selfish Gene* is a book on evolution by Richard Dawkins published in 1976.

It expresses a gene-centred view of evolution. Evolution is best viewed as acting on genes. Selection at the level of organisms or populations almost never overrides selection based on genes. The contention is that the genes that get passed on are the ones whose consequences serve their own implicit interests. Consequently, populations tend towards a strategy that is stable in evolutionary terms.

The Selfish Gene is a catchy and memorable title, but is not particularly useful. Andrew Brown has written, in *The Science of Selfishness* (1998):

> 'Selfish', when applied to genes, doesn't mean 'selfish' at all. It means, instead, an extremely important quality for which there is no good word in the English language: 'the quality of being copied by a Darwinian selection process.' This is a complicated mouthful. There ought to be a better, shorter word—but 'selfish' isn't it.

8   One of Geddes's more memorable quotes is: 'I can't and won't keep accounts.' His father was a very different kettle of fish, demonstrating all the peacetime virtues of an Army Quartermaster.

MS 10605 in the National Library of Scotland is a collection of documents pertaining to Alexander Geddes, father of Patrick Geddes. In a very neat school exercise book he entered his 'Particulars of Income for the year ending 31 March 1897'.

His total income for the year had been £295 – 18 – 9d. He was in receipt of two pensions, one in respect of 20 plus years service in the Black Watch, and the other for 20 plus years of officer service in the Perthshire Rifles, the equivalent of the Territorial Army of today. In addition he had an annuity of £15 per annum 'for meritorious service'.

Almost as much income again came from investments, mainly in Australia, Canada and New Zealand. One son had emigrated to New Zealand, where he prospered. Another had married a general's daughter and become a successful banker. Their combined advice must have been helpful in placing Alexander's capital. £28 came from Patrick Geddes – Father must have been foolish – or loyal – enough to have invested in one of his son's ventures and this was the interest on the capital lent. (In 1892 Patrick Geddes had written of his Garden Village project in Roseburn, Edinburgh: 'Here is another of my as yet disastrous yet not ill-conceived endeavours.')

9   'Pullars of Perth' were 'the largest and best equipped cleaning and dyeing works in the world'. (C.A. Oakley, *Scottish Industry Today*, The Moray Press, Edinburgh, 1937)

10   There are occasions when Geddes seems to be deliberately trying to be difficult. 'Asymptotic' refers to the diminishing distance between a straight line and a plane curve as they approach infinity. 'Self-regarding' is the struggle for life, the survival of the fittest, while 'other-regarding' – love – was 'creation's final law'. This optimistic view could only have been shaken by the First World War.

11   H.G. Wells (1866–1946), 'The Father of Science Fiction' and another alumnus of the Royal School of Mines, was a basically optimistic writer who was changed by World War 1 – his last book was *Mind at the End of its Tether*.

Others had worse wars than Geddes. He spent most of the war in India, where his wife died just after his favoured older son Alistair was killed on the Western Front. His Cities Exhibition was sunk by enemy action on its way to India. After the war, Geddes continued to work with remarkable intensity and freshness (see An Evolution Chronology).

An Evolution Chronology

DARWIN'S LIFE WAS LONG and complex, as were the lives of many around him who contributed to The Evolution of Evolution. Fitting them all into one vast timeline does, however, serve to show up the connections between the contributors and the extent to which one generation fed upon another.

Those new to Darwin will find all the basic facts they need below. Old Darwinists may find some interesting connections and juxtapositions. For example, note how 1797 and 1882 could be seen as, respectively, a coincidence and a turning point, in their different ways. In 1882 Darwin died. This could be seen as the end of the Paleolithic in Evolution, during which it had been taken from crude beginnings to a fair degree of sophistication. In the same year, Walther Flemming of the University of Kiel, in Germany, discovered what would later be called chromosomes. He went on to study cell division and the distribution of chromosomes in the nuclei of cells.

Like Darwin, Flemming was unaware of Mendel's work, so it was another 20 years before the connection was made between Flemming's discoveries and genetic inheritance. Reference to 1902, 1940, 1944, 1962, 1990, 2000 and 2003 in the chronology below will show how our knowledge and understanding of life itself has been deepened and widened.

In the interests of brevity I have used initials to identify the key figures in the Evolution of Evolution, as follows:

R.C. – Robert Chambers, C.D. – Charles Darwin, P.G. – Patrick Geddes, J.H. – James Hutton, C.L. – Charles Lyell

1788	J.H. leads a field excursion to Siccar Point.
1795	*Theory of the Earth,* by J.H., published.
1797	Death of J.H.
	C.L. born at Kinnordy House, Kirriemuir.
1802	R.C. born at Peebles.
1809	C.D. born Shrewsbury, 12 February, same day as Abraham Lincoln. In this year also, Lamarck, in *La Philosophie zoologique,* put forward the notion of transmutation of species.

1817	C.D. at school in Shrewsbury. Death of mother.
1824	C.L. visits Siccar Point with Sir James Hall.
1825	C.D. enrolled in Faculty of Medicine in Edinburgh.
1827	Brief stay in Paris. C.D. quit Edinburgh.
1828	C.D.'s father enrolled him at Christ's College, Cambridge, with the intention of his going into the Church.
1830	Publication of *Principles of Geology,* by C.L.
1831	In January C.D. received degree of BA. On 27 December left England on board the *Beagle.* C.L appointed to Chair of Geology, King's College, London.
1832	*Chambers Edinburgh Journal* started.
1835	On 15 January C.D. observed volcanic eruption in Chile. On 20 February he witnessed an earthquake.
1836	*Beagle* returned to England, 2 October. C.D. settled in London.
1837	Victoria crowned queen of England (*sic*). On 23 March C.D. saw an orang-outang for the first time. Began his first file on 'transmutation of species'.
1838	Publication of *Elements of Geology,* by C.L.
1839	29 January, C.D. married his first cousin Emma Wedgwood. First child, William, born December. C.D. met Joseph Hooker, botanist, who became his best friend.
1840	Meeting of British Association in Glasgow. Agassiz in Scotland.
1841	Birth of C.D.'s oldest daughter, Annie. C.L. visits America.
1842	Darwin family move to Down House, in Kent, where C.D. will live for the rest of his life.
1844	Anonymous publication of *Vestiges of Creation.*
1845	Publication of *Travels in North America,* by C.L. C.L.'s second visit to America. Anonymous publication of *Explanations: A Sequel to the 'Vestiges'.*
1847	C.D. begins his work on barnacles, which will last eight years. British Association meeting at Oxford. R.C. publicly humiliated.

1848   Death of C.D.'s father. C.D. inherits considerable fortune.
        Can support his family and concentrate on his scientific
        work.
        R.C. visits Glen Roy.
        Publication of *Ancient Sea Margins,* by R.C.
1849   Publication of *A Second Visit to the United States of
        North America,* by C.L.
1851   Death of Annie, C.D.'s favourite daughter, on 22 April.
        Publication of *Tracings of the North of Europe,* by R.C.
1853   First lifesize dinosaur model shown by palaeontologists
        near London on 31 December.
1854   P.G. born 2 October, in Ballater, youngest of five children.
1856   Discovery in Germany of the first bones of Neanderthal
        man, (*Homo neanderthalensis*) arousing controversy.
        Publication of *Tracings in Iceland and the Faroe Islands,*
        by R.C.
1857   C.D. awarded medal of the Royal Society, confirming his
        standing as a biologist.
1857   P.G.'s family moved to Mount Tabor, Perth.
1858   Death of Charles Waring, C.D.'s youngest son. Friends
        of Darwin set up lectures by Darwin and Wallace before
        the Linnaean Society.
1859   24 November, publication of *Origin of Species.* 1,250
        copies sold on first day.
        Chambers Encyclopaedia first published.
1860   Thomas Huxley defends C.D.'s ideas against the Bishop of
        Oxford, 'Soapy Sam', in a legendary verbal boxing match.
1862   Publication of *On the Fertilisation of Orchids by Insects.*
1863   Publication of *The Antiquity of Man,* by C.L. (his last
        book).
1865   Publication of *The Movements and Habits of Climbing
        Plants.*
1868   Publication of *The Variation of Animals and Plants under
        Domestication.*
        Discovery of the remains of our Cro-Magnon ancestor in
        the Dordogne.
1869   The biologist Friedrich Miescher isolates the cell of a
        substance which will later be called DNA.

1871   Publication of *The Descent of Man, and Selection in Relation to Sex.*
Death of R.C.
P.G. left Perth Academy for work in bank and 'free home studies'.

1872   Publication of *The Expression of the Emotions in Man and Animals* which forms the basis of modern ethnography.

1874   P.G. studies biology at Edinburgh (one week) and London (under Huxley).

1875   Publication of *Carnivorous Plants.*
Death of C.L. Buried in Westminster Abbey.

1878   P.G. at Roscoff (Brittany) and the Sorbonne.

1879   P.G. set up Scottish Zoological Station at Cowie, Stonehaven.
The Mexican Adventure.
Discovery of cave paintings of Altamira.

1880   Publication of *The Various Contrivances by which Orchids are Fertilised by Insects.*
P.G., Demonstrator in Botany, Edinburgh University.

1881   Publication of *The Formation of Vegetable Mould, through the Action of Worms, with Observations on their Habits.*

1882   Letter from C.D. to P.G.
C.D.'s death on 19 April, at Down House, after having whispered to Emma: 'I am not afraid of dying.' Buried in Westminster Abbey, London, not far from the tomb of Isaac Newton.
Walther Flemming discovered chromosomes.

After Darwin

1884   Twelfth edition of *Vestiges of Creation* published.
Authorship of R.C. revealed.

1886   P.G.'s marriage to Anna Morton.

1887   P.G.'s daughter Norah born.
University Hall, first self-governing hostel.

1887–1900 P.G. set up and run Summer Schools every August.

1888	P.G., Professor of Botany, University College, Dundee.
1891	P.G.'s son, Alasdair, born.
1892	P.G. started Outlook Tower.
1893	P.G. created Ramsay Gardens as co-operative flats.
1895	P.G.'s son, Arthur, born.
1897	P.G. in Cyprus – survey and planning.
1900	P.G. held International Assembly at *Exposition Universelle,* Paris
	P.G.'s first visit to United States.
	Several scientists rediscover Mendel's work on heredity.
1901	P.G.'s return visit to United States.
1902	Theodor Boveri and Walter Sutton advance the notion that the mechanisms for heredity are to be found in the chromosomes.
1903	P.G. Dunfermline development plan and publication of *City Development.*
1908	P.G. relocated and restored Crosby Hall (Chelsea) as residence for university women.
1910	P.G.'s Cities Exhibition at Chelsea (then toured till lost at sea 1914).
1913	P.G.'s Cities Exhibition awarded Grand Prix in Ghent.
1914–15	P.G.'s first visit to India (with Alasdair).
1915	*Cities in Evolution* published.
1915–17	P.G.'s second visit to India (with Anna).
1917	Deaths of Alasdair and Anna.
1919	P.G.'s Retirement and Farewell Lecture (Dundee).
	Planning in Jerusalem and Tel Aviv.
	Professor of Civics and Sociology at Bombay.
1919–23	P.G.'s third visit to India (with Arthur).
1923	P.G.'s third visit to USA.
1924	P.G. left Bombay for Montpellier (health reasons).
	Collège des Écossais founded (by P.G.).
1925	At Dayton (Tennessee) the first 'monkey trial' of a teacher guilty, according to the law of Tennessee, of having taught evolution. He was fined 100 dollars, but the law was ridiculed and the fine was never paid.
	Civil List pension of £80 awarded to P.G.

1926	Compensation of £2000 paid to P.G. for loss of Cities Exhibition.
	P.G.'s plan for city of Tel Aviv accepted.
1928	P.G.'s marriage to Lilian Brown.
1932	Offer of knighthood accepted by P.G. – accolade 25 February.
	Death at Montpellier – 17 April.
1940	Discovery of the Lascaux caves. In the '40s was elaborated Neo-Darwinism, the biological impossibility of the inheritance of acquired characteristics.
1944	The molecular biologist Oswald Avery identifies DNA as the hereditary component of chromosomes.
1956	Frank Fraser Darling published *Pelican in the Wilderness: A Naturalist's Odyssey in North America*.
1959	Mary and Louis Leakey discover the first *Australopithecus*.
1962	Crick, Watson and Wilkins receive the Nobel Prize for the discovery of the double helix structure of DNA. Rosalind Franklin, the photographer, was forgotten by history.
1962	*Silent Spring* – Rachel Carson.
1964	The primatologist Jane Goodall reveals to the world that chimpanzees make use of tools.
1968	A judgment of the Supreme Court of the United States annuls a law forbidding the teaching of evolution.
1969	Reith Lectures – *Wilderness and Plenty* (Frank Fraser Darling).
1972	*Blueprint for Survival* (*The Ecologist*).
1973	Establishment of Sir Patrick Geddes Memorial Trust. 'Geddes-awareness' campaign started by *Bulletin of Environmental Education*.
1974	Discovery of the fossilised remains of the *Australopithecus* Lucy.
	Small is Beautiful: Economics as if People Mattered – E.F. Schumacher.
1975	*A Most Unsettling Person* – Paddy Kitchen.
1978	*The Worlds of Patrick Geddes* – Patrick Boardman.
1982	Second 'Monkey Trial' at Little Rock (Arkansas). The creationists' case is dismissed.

	Commemorative P.G. events in several locations, home and abroad.
1985	Patrick Geddes Centre for Planning Studies set up (in the Outlook Tower).
1990	Beginning of the sequencing of the human genome. *Patrick Geddes: Social Evolutionist and City Planner* – Helen Meller.
1991–92	International Summer Meetings run by Patrick Geddes Centre.
1992	Rio Earth Summit and Local Agenda 21.
2000	The complete sequencing of the fly *Drosophila* is published.
2003	Complete sequencing of the human genome. Discovery of Florès man (*Homo floresiensis*).
2004	Geddes Garden at Scots College, Montpellier, restored. *Ideas in Evolution* – Geddes 150th Anniversary Symposium, Edinburgh. *Patrick Geddes: The Regeneration of Edinburgh* – Anniversary Exhibition at the Matthew Gallery, University of Edinburgh. *Think Global, Act Local: The Life and Legacy of Patrick Geddes* – Walter Stephen (ed).
2005	Third 'Monkey Trial' at Dover (Pennsylvania). A Federal tribunal interdicts the issue of a manual promoting 'intelligent design' to public establishments.
2007	A creationist atlas published in Turkey is disseminated to educational establishments in several European countries. The enemies targeted by the authors are Darwin and Darwinists. Death of the monkey Washoe at the age of 42 years. She was the first monkey to learn sign language. She knew 250 words, some of which she transmitted to Loulis, her adopted son. Today, other animals know thousands of signs.
2008	In September the Church of England conceded that it was over-defensive and over-emotional in dismissing C.D.'s ideas and said that present 'anti-evolutionary fervour' was 'an indictment on the Church.'

2009   Bicentenary of the birth of C.D. On his birthday the Vatican declared that C.D.'s theory of evolution was compatible with Christian faith, 'and could even be traced to St Augustine and St Thomas Aquinas.'
C.D.'s theory is still a centre for debate in science, philosophy and theology.
C.D.'s importance has not diminished.

Appendix – Extract from
Who's Who – 1930

GEDDES, PATRICK, late Professor of Sociology and Civics, University of Bombay; Professor of Botany (retired), Univ. College, Dundee (St Andrews Univ.); Senior Resident of Univ. Hall, Edinburgh; Director of the Cities and Town Planning Exhibition; b. 1854; y.s. of late Capt. Alex. Geddes; m. 1st, 1886, Anna (d. 1917), e.d. of Frazer Morton, merchant, Liverpool; two s. one d.; 2nd, 1928, Lilian, 2nd d. of late John Armour Brown, Moredun, Paisley. Educ.: Perth Academy, Royal School of Mines, University Coll., London; Sorbonne; Univs. Of Edinburgh, Montpellier etc. Successively Demonstrator of Physiology at Univ. Coll., London; of Zoology at Univ. at Aberdeen; of Botany at Edinburgh; Lecturer on Natural History in School of Medicine, Edinburgh; with intervals of travel, e.g. exploration in Mexico, visits to Continental universities, zoo-logical stations, and botanic gardens, as also to Cyprus and the East, to USA etc. *Studies:* geography, biology, history, art, social economy and civics. Educational work (besides teaching) mainly in organisation of University Halls, Edinburgh and Chelsea, each as a beginning of colle-giate life, e.g. at Edinburgh, with its Summer Meeting and Outlook Tower. This is a regional, geographic, and synthetic type-museum, with associated undertakings of geotechnic and social purpose e.g. city improve-ment (Old Edinburgh, etc.), gardens, parks etc. Publishing house (Geddes and Colleagues) associated with Celtic and general literature and art, with geography, education and synthetics. Actively occupied in city improvement, town-planning, and educational initiatives at home, on continent and in India, etc. and with University designs (India, Jerusalem, etc), and development of Cite Universitaire Mediterraneanne at Montpellier. *Publications:* Evolution of Sex, Evolution, Sex, Biology and Life in Evolution (jointly with Prof. J. Arthur Thomson); Chapters in Modern Botany; City Development; Cities in Evolution; The Life and Work of Sir Jagadis C. Bose, FRS, 1920; The Coming Polity (with V.V. Branford); Ideas at War (with Prof. Gilbert Slater); Our Social Inheritance (with V.V. Branford), etc. *Recreations:* gardening, rambling. *Address:* Outlook Tower, Univ. Hall, Edinburgh; c/o Sociological Society, Leplay House, 65 Belgrave Road, sw1; Collège des Ecossais, Montpellier, France.

(For further information use www.patrickgeddestrust.co.uk)

Further Reading

THERE IS A DARWIN INDUSTRY and books about Darwin are almost as numerous as the letters Darwin wrote in his lifetime – and they amount to over 12,000! The bibliography is vast – for example, Marc Giraud lists over 100 titles in French – and fills the subconscious.

The following have been consulted recently in connection with this project. All are readable, interesting and almost entirely accurate.

Cyril Aydon: *Charles Darwin* (Constable, London, 2002)

Stephen Baxter: *Revolutions in the Earth* (Weidenfeld & Nicolson, London, 2003)

Janet Browne & Michael Neve (eds): *Voyage of the Beagle* (Penguin Books, Harmondsworth, 1989)

Robert Chambers LLD: *Traditions of Edinburgh* (W.&R. Chambers Ltd, London and Edinburgh, 1868)

Robert Chambers Esq, FRSE: *Ancient Sea Margins* (W.&R. Chambers, Edinburgh, 1868)

Charles Darwin: *The Expression of the Emotions in Man and Animals* (John Murray, London, 1872)

Adrian Desmond & James Moore: *Darwin* (Michael Joseph, London, 1991)

Adrian Desmond & James Moore: *Darwin's Sacred Cause* (Allen Lane, London, 2009)

Marc Giraud: *Darwin, c'est tout bête* (Robert Laffont, Paris, 2009)

Charles Lyell: *Principles of Geology* (Penguin Books, London, 1997)

Alan McKirdy, John Gordon & Roger Crofts: *Land of Mountain and Flood: The Geology and Landforms of Scotland* (Birlinn, Edinburgh, 2007)

G.H. Mitchell, E.K. Walton and Douglas Grant (eds): *Edinburgh Geology: An Excursion Guide* (Oliver and Boyd, Edinburgh and London, 1960)

Duncan M Porter & Peter W. Graham: *The Portable Darwin* (Penguin Books, Harmondsworth, 1993)

James A Secord: *Victorian Sensation* (University of Chicago Press, 2000)

The *Darwin Correspondence Project* www.darwinproject.ac.uk/darwinletters is a double miracle:

> of modern technology, in making a vast body of information (one of Darwin's favourite words) accessible to millions, and of industry and organisation, allowing us a glimpse into the life and methods of the one-man database that was Darwin.

For Geddes, the following can be regarded as the 'basic kit'.

Philip Boardman: *The Worlds of Patrick Geddes* (Routledge and KeganPaul, 1978)

Amelia Defries: *The Interpreter Geddes: The Man and His Gospel* (Routledge, London 1927)

Gifford, MacWilliam and Walker: *The Buildings of Scotland: Edinburgh*, (Penguin Books Ltd, 1984)

Paddy Kitchen: *A Most Unsettling Person* (Victor Gollancz, London, 1975)

Sofia Leonard: 'The Regeneration of the Old Town of Edinburgh by Patrick Geddes', (*Planning History* Vol 21 No 2, February 1999)

Murdo Macdonald (ed): 'Patrick Geddes: Ecologist, Educator. Visual Thinker' (*Edinburgh Review*, Issue 88, Summer 1992)

Murdo Macdonald: *A Democratic Intellect* (awaiting publication).

Kenneth MacLean & Walter Stephen (eds): *Exploration* (Hills of Home, Edinburgh, 2007)

Philip Mairet: *The Life and Letters of Patrick Geddes* (Lund Humphries, London, 1957)

Helen Meller: *Patrick Geddes, Social Evolutionist and City Planner,* (Routledge, London, 1990)

Walter Stephen (ed): *Think Global, Act Local: The Life and Legacy of Patrick Geddes* (Luath Press, Edinburgh, 2004)

Walter Stephen (ed): *A Vigorous Institution: The Living Legacy of Patrick Geddes* (Luath Press, Edinburgh, 2007)

Walter Stephen: *Where was Patrick Geddes born? The Last Word?* (Hills of Home, Edinburgh, 2008)

A full Geddes bibliography can be found on the Sir Patrick Geddes Memorial Trust website: For further information use www.patrickgeddestrust.co.uk

Index

A Vigorous Institution: The Living Legacy of Patrick Geddes

Edited by Walter Stephen

ISBN 1 905222 88 2 PBK £12.99

Patrick Geddes was an original thinker and innovator, an internationalist steeped in Scottishness. His achievements included conservation projects in the Old Town of Edinburgh and in London; community development through greening the urban environment; and plans for Dunfermline, Cyprus, Tel Aviv and over 50 Indian cities. His Outlook Tower was the 'world's first sociological laboratory'. He pioneered summer schools and self-governing student hostels, used public art to stimulate social change, and established his own College of Art in Edinburgh and a Collège des Écossais in Montpellier.

A Vigorous Institution brings together a team of many talents to take a fresh look at Geddes and his place in the world today. Can he still be seen as a vigorous institution in the 21st century? What is his influence on planning policies in the new, devolved Scotland? Why do his ideas resonate still in Japan, India and Catalunya?

Aspects of his life are re-examined in an attempt to understand further his thinking. How much of an anarchist was he? How influential were his home and childhood experiences? Why did he change his name and why – till the publication of this book – was his birthhouse shrouded in mystery?

Think Global, Act Local
The Life and Legacy of Patrick Geddes

Edited by Walter Stephen

ISBN 1 84282 079 6 PBK £12.99

Town planning. Interest-led, open-minded education. Preservation of buildings with historical worth. Community gardens. All are so central to modern society that our age tends to claim these notions as its own. In fact they were first visualised by Sir Patrick Geddes, a largely forgotten Victorian Scot and one of the greatest forward thinkers in history.

Gardener, biologist, conservationist, social evolutionist, peace warrior, and town planner, Geddes spent many years conserving and restoring Edinburgh's historic Royal Mile at a time when most decaying buildings were simply torn down. With renovation came educational ideas such as the development of the Outlook Tower, numerous summer schools and his Collège des Écossais in Montpellier. In India much of Geddes's belief in people planning can be seen, taking the form of pedestrian zones, student accommodation for women, and urban diversification projects.

The Art of Putting

Willie Park Junior
ISBN 1 905222 66 1 PBK £5.99

'The man who can putt is a match for anyone.' So said Willie Park in 1920. It is still true today. Willie Park's transcendent manual seeks to share the methods which made him 'the best and most consistent putter in the world'. Equipment may have changed and competition become fiercer, but with Park's guidance, you too will have a fighting chance of making that all-important putt.

This guide to putting for players of all skill levels is fully illustrated; covers every aspect of putting, from grip to the lie of the green; and is a clear, concise and detailed guide to mastery of technique.

The Game of Golf

Willie Park Junior
ISBN 1 905222 65 3 HBK £12.99

The golfer in Willie Park Junior speaks out and voices his opinions on golfing equipment and techniques. Straight from the man who brought golf from Scotland to the world comes a comprehensive guide to playing golf that complements the game of players of all skill levels.

Every aspect of playing, from selecting equipment to proper swing and grip, is explained in detail and given beside the opinion and tips of a successful 19th century golf champion. This commentary reveals the finer details of the game and original techniques that can still be applied today. Including a helpful glossary and diagrams and illustrations, the history and art of golf are revealed.

Willie Park Junior: The Man Who Took Golf To The World

Walter Stephen

ISBN 1 905222 21 1 HBK £25.00

In the 19th century Musselburgh, Scotland was a hotbed of golfing genius. The local links produced five Open Champions, and of these golfing greats, Willie Park Junior was undoubtedly more than just a good golfer. Park redefined the image of the golf professional and took the game from being an esoteric pastime, practised in a few favoured localities, to its present status as a worldwide game.

Twice winner of the Open, Park also played challenge and demonstration matches at home and abroad. His career in golf course design took him from Britain to Western Europe and then North America; in total Park laid out over 160 courses world-wide, over 40 of these in the United States and more than 20 in Canada, many of which are still in use today.

After a century of improved golf technology – better clubs, a larger ball, and more tailored course layouts – what legacy has Willie Park Junior left to the modern golfer? Walter Stephen tours us round some of Park's best-loved courses to see how they have stood the tests of time and tee-off.

a book that is quirky, idiosyncratic, frustrating and ultimately as fascinating as the game itself.
THE HERALD

Wild Lives: A Herd of Red Deer

Frank Fraser Darling

ISBN 1 906307 42 3 PBK £9.99

Frank Fraser Darling was an ecologist, a conservationist, and a prophet. He was the first naturalist to leave the laboratory and the library to spend long periods observing and recording our largest land mammal in its mountain habitat – our last great wilderness. The David Attenborough of his day, Fraser Darling inspired a generation to follow in his footsteps, and to love natural history and the Highlands.

A Herd of Red Deer is the result of two years spent in one of the most hostile environments in the British Isles, following the seasonal wanderings of the deer through the fly season, the rut, facing the winter and rearing fawns in the spring. Fraser Darling studies changes in the herds to build up a moving and emotive picture of the life of the red deer.

Details of these and other books published by Luath Press can be found at:
www.luath.co.uk

Luath Press Limited
committed to publishing well written books worth reading

LUATH PRESS takes its name from Robert Burns, whose little collie Luath (*Gael.*, swift or nimble) tripped up Jean Armour at a wedding and gave him the chance to speak to the woman who was to be his wife and the abiding love of his life. Burns called one of 'The Twa Dogs' Luath after Cuchullin's hunting dog in Ossian's *Fingal*. Luath Press was established in 1981 in the heart of Burns country, and is now based a few steps up the road from Burns' first lodgings on Edinburgh's Royal Mile.
Luath offers you distinctive writing with a hint of unexpected pleasures.

Most bookshops in the UK, the US, Canada, Australia, New Zealand and parts of Europe either carry our books in stock or can order them for you. To order direct from us, please send a £sterling cheque, postal order, international money order or your credit card details (number, address of cardholder and expiry date) to us at the address below. Please add post and packing as follows: UK – £1.00 per delivery address; overseas surface mail – £2.50 per delivery address; overseas airmail – £3.50 for the first book to each delivery address, plus £1.00 for each additional book by airmail to the same address. If your order is a gift, we will happily enclose your card or message at no extra charge.

Luath Press Limited
543/2 Castlehill
The Royal Mile
Edinburgh EH1 2ND
Scotland
Telephone: 0131 225 4326 (24 hours)
Fax: 0131 225 4324
email: sales@luath.co.uk
Website: www.luath.co.uk